"This book is an excellent primer for those interested in and burdened for church planting in the African-American context. It will provide the reader with a necessary foundation for planting biblically based churches in the African-American community."

—Tony Evans,
Oak Cliff Bible Fellowship,
Dallas, TX

"This book is well written and speaks to a serious need in the African community. We need a guide like this to help us plant churches and then provide the resources to sustain them. I consider this book a major contribution to the whole idea of church in general."

—Dr. Fred C. Lofton,
Pastor of Metropolitan Baptist Church,
Memphis, TN

"This is a much-needed book. It would be great to see it in the hands of every seminary graduate who feels led of God to organize or pastor a church. I also recommend this book as a must-read by pastors, especially those with associate ministers in their churches who need counsel in this area."

—Dr. Lloyd C. Blue,
Executive Director of Church Growth Unlimited,
Mendenhall, MS

CHURCH PLANTING

IN THE AFRICAN-AMERICAN CONTEXT

CHURCH PLANTING

IN THE african-american context

shape a vision – plan wisely
know your community – lead effectively
reach families – transcend ethnic boundaries

HOZELL C. FRANCIS

ZondervanPublishingHouse
Grand Rapids, Michigan

A Division of HarperCollinsPublishers

Church Planting in the African-American Context
Copyright © 1999 by Hozell C. Francis

Requests for information should be addressed to:

Zondervan Publishing House
Grand Rapids, Michigan 49530

Library of Congress Cataloging-in-Publication Data

Francis, Hozell C., 1949–
    Church planting in the African-American context / Hozell C. Francis.
      p.   cm.
    Includes bibliographical references.
    ISBN 0-310-22877-8 (softcover)
    1. Church development, New.   2. Afro-American churches.   I. Title.
BV652.24.F73 1999
254'.1'08996073—dc21   99-18863
                                                    CIP

Interior design by Sherri L. Hoffman

Printed in the United States of America

---

99 00 01 02 03 04 05 06 /❖ DC/ 10 9 8 7 6 5 4 3 2 1

This work is dedicated to my loving wife, Lynda. She has been my confidante, supporter, and inspiration since 1980. And to Jack and Alger Francis, my parents.

contents

Acknowledgments   11

1. A Different World   13

2. How African-American Churches Are Planted   23

3. Why African-American Churches Are
   Different From Anglo Churches   35

4. Leadership in African-American Churches   43

5. Ministry in African-American Churches   53

6. Contemporary Preaching in African-American
   Churches   61

7. Mission Emphases of African-American
   Churches   69

8. Sociological Perspectives of the
   African-American Church   75

9. Economic Factors in African-American
   Churches   81

10. The Hostility Factor in the African-American
    Community   89

11. The Homogeneous Principle in African-American
    Churches   97

12. The Future of Church Planting in
    African-American Churches   105

Bibliography   115

Notes   119

acknowLeDGments

I would like to thank some of the many people who inspired me to write this book. Dr. Whalen S. Jones, my pastor and spiritual father, has encouraged me both by word and by example. He shows what it means to be a true servant of the Lord. Dr. Gary McIntosh and Dr. Mick Boersma, both professors at Talbot School of Theology, have been models for me. Their proofreading and suggestions made this a better book. Dr. McIntosh also taught me how to prepare a book manuscript and market it.

I also want to thank Althea R. Brown, my typist and reader. She was of immense help in getting the technical aspects of the book in order. I thank the people of Emmaus Baptist Church, my first church plant. This church was the basis of my initial practice as a church planter and offered a myriad of experiences.

Special regards are expressed to Dr. Tony Evans of Oak Cliff Bible Fellowship in Dallas, Texas, who took the time to critique the manuscript before I submitted it for publication. His feedback was highly regarded and helpful. Thanks to Dr. Lloyd C. Blue of Church Growth Unlimited in Mendenhall, Mississippi, and to Ms. and Dr. Fred C. Lofton of Metropolitan Baptist Church in Memphis, Tennessee. They also took the time and effort to review the manuscript, and their comments and suggestions were appreciated.

Finally, immeasurable credit goes to my devoted wife, Lynda, and our three children, Hozell, Haili, and Shawna.

They gave me the liberty required to research and write this book. We rejoiced and agonized together during its preparation. Without their sacrifice and support, this book would still be just an idea.

Chapter One

a
DIfferent
worLd

There is neither Jew nor Greek, slave nor free, male nor female, for you are all one in Christ Jesus.

—Galatians 3:28

good intentions, good model

In the story "Beauty and the Beast," Beauty, to save her father's life, agrees to reside at an enchanted castle with the Beast. Although very fearful of the Beast and terrified by his appearance, Beauty is eventually able to see beyond his monstrous appearance into his heart. Considering the Beast's kind and generous nature, her perception of his appearance changes. Beauty is no longer repelled by the way he looks; instead, she is drawn to his loving nature. The better she gets to know him, the less monstrous he seems. Finally, finding him dying of a broken heart, she reveals her love for him, thus transforming the Beast into a handsome prince. Not only do they live happily ever after, but all those who happen into their domain in despair are changed, finding on their departure that their hearts are now filled with goodness and beauty.

As in this often-told story, we are usually repelled by those we do not know. However, when we become friends, we do not understand how once they seemed so monstrous to us. Nowhere is the story of Beauty and the Beast more apparent than in intercultural and interracial relations.

When people hail from different cultures and backgrounds, clashes are inevitable. People who are from similar backgrounds will often express uneasiness when put in close proximity to one another. Even when serious efforts are proffered in order to diminish tension, it still finds a way to express itself. Although intercultural expressions are often considered debasing and counterproductive, social conflicts can be useful in bringing about constructive change.

Remember that in the early church it didn't take long before the Hellenists found occasion to protest against the inequities that they thought the native Hebrews were guilty of. In this instance, the problem was properly addressed by responsible leadership. In fact, it led to further official policy-making in the church regarding the relative duties and the division of labor among those in service. The church can be a model of building good relationships between people groups. It has the model and capacity to do so if its leaders are willing to be directive. However, church leaders from both the black and the white churches appear to be content to ignore the complaints and charges of the people. Apparently it is safer to downgrade and even deny the differences that exist between our cultures than to acknowledge them. The good intention is to avoid trouble and conflict. Yet when matters are dealt with in an honest and forthright manner, people can appreciate the candor even if they do not agree with a given position.

The history of the sons of Europe differs significantly from that of the sons of Africa. I state this fact without attempting to attribute a value judgment in this connection.

On the continents of our origins many differences existed. There were religious, agricultural, climatic, political, economic, and social differences. These various aspects of human life all make up a people's culture. When people have different cultures, they will have different worldviews. They simply will not see eye to eye. Some of this will be mitigated by cultural assimilation after several generations. However, when cultural assimilation is inhibited, an incomplete acculturation is virtually assured. So, given our different points of origin, the historical background of blacks and whites in America is inherently different.

The different worlds that we live in have been effectively maintained by social and political sanctions. It does not take long before a child learns that we are from different worlds. The environment portrays it. Until recent decades, and still today, though to a lesser extent, we generally have had separate communities, schools, recreation, churches, and the like so that all of our children were naturally inculcated with a knowledge of the different worlds in which we exist.

When I was six years old, I began school. I can still remember having to walk about four miles from my house on a rural dirt road to a bus stop on the main highway. It was the same whether in rain, snow, hail, or sleet. Yet I had to come to terms with the fact that another bus would drive off the main highway to pick up each white student, door to door. I cannot tell you how many times their bus drove past me in the cold and rain. How could they not see themselves as being different from me and me from them when social convention had built the distinctions into the very fibers of society at every level?

The kinds of experiences that we have help to determine who we are and how we view the world.

When people believe that they are different and have what they perceive to be justifications for such belief, their behavior will be consistent with their beliefs. The challenge that the church faces is to bridge the gap that exists between people groups. With some creativity, this can be done on many levels. One of the most impressive national efforts is the Promise Keepers ministry. This ministry was founded by ex–football coach Bill McCartney of the University of Colorado several years ago. He has consistently challenged Christian men to seek racial reconciliation. He clearly understands that there is a problem that the Christian community needs to address when it comes to the differences and tensions of race relations. I had the privilege of being at Promise Keepers 1994 in Anaheim, California. McCartney's passion and sense of integrity were quite moving. If we are to experience positive movement in uniting God's people in kingdom-building enterprises, passionate leaders must take charge in leading the people to more enlightened attitudes. African-Americans in particular and the majority of church leaders in general must be willing to develop systems that are mutually beneficial to social and religious elevation.

> THE CHALLENGE THAT THE CHURCH FACES IS TO BRIDGE THE GAP THAT EXISTS BETWEEN PEOPLE GROUPS. WITH SOME CREATIVITY, THIS CAN BE DONE ON MANY LEVELS.

APPRECIATING OUR DIFFERENCES

Instead of cursing the differences, we must applaud and capitalize on them. Diversity can represent strength. As I said, Bill McCartney recognizes the different worlds that we have come from. Yet he is building toward connecting the different parts like a mosaic. As believers we are to encourage, challenge, and equip one another for Christian service. At the final session of Promise Keepers 1993 McCartney exclaimed,

> The time has come! We have been in a war but not at war! If we are to make a difference, it will require much more than we've been doing until now. While we have been sleeping in our routines, the enemy has attacked relentlessly, cutting away the spiritual heritage of America. If we don't respond now, time could run out![1]

Amen! We must be willing to put aside preconceived notions about people and advance meaningful approaches to multicultural projects.

The problem with not acknowledging differences, both overt and subtle ones, is that we will not attempt to correct what we do not perceive to be broken. A most startling awakening for me occurred when I was about ten years old. My mother and I were walking past a farmhouse when a little white boy about five years old said, "Look, Mom, some Niggers!" I still vividly recall how my mother and I totally ignored them and acted as though nothing was ever said. I can't remember that we ever made any mention of the remark. However, our failure, fear, or lack of skill to deal with the feelings that we both must have had did nothing to alleviate the matter. If we do not learn to handle our differences in respectable and responsible ways, we will all suffer to some degree.

There are numerous areas where blacks and whites have similar aspirations. For example, most of us desire success in our careers, and we want our children to grow up and make a contribution to society; we are concerned about owning our homes and growing up spiritually. Conversely, there are generalized differences between blacks and whites. Often there are measurable variations in music appreciation, art, dance, vernacular, dress, etc. Evidently these differences have their origin in our histories. Nevertheless, they affect the way we are and act in every aspect of life. The church is not immune to these distinctives. Indeed, they are evident in many facets of church life. It is conceivable that there will be a continuing market for the individualized expression of the differences we have. However, a significant number of persons can be equipped to work in tandem for progress and to go beyond the confines of cultural restraints.

In order to aspire to new levels of intercultural mutuality we must dare to dream the impossible and the improbable. In 1963 Martin Luther King had a dream that "one day ... little black boys and black girls will be able to join hands with little white boys and white girls and walk together as sisters and brothers."[2] The fact that such a dream was necessary is itself indicative of the stress that race relations have experienced in America. Moreover, it would be interesting to discover how much progress we have made in that direction today. The benefits of improved interaction between black and white America are many. Most important is that it signals to the world that the Christian church is indeed genuine and powerful. The model of the body of Christ working together to His glory in spite of our differences is a persuasive one.

If indeed we are one in Christ, we the people of Christ should be able to overcome the divisiveness that sometimes springs from our differences. In order to plant viable churches in the African-American communities, we need well-trained and Spirit-filled ministers. The training that future Christian workers in urban America receive must be comprehensive in nature. It should contain context-specific training that will enable Christian ministers to apply pertinent solutions to problems they encounter. The contemporary urban church is beset with some unique circumstances. Surely, the epidemic levels of the homeless, the unemployed, the diseased, the mentally ill, and the criminal element all work against the prosperity of church-planting enterprises. In addition, there is the ever-increasing presence of cults, such as Black Muslims, that further confuses the issues.

The attempt to plant churches at any place can be met with obstacles. It is the degree and depth of the obstacles that the church planter in the contemporary African-American context must be mindful of. Even though many obstacles do exist, many black churches are growing very rapidly. In Los Angeles alone there are several churches with memberships in the multiple thousands—for example, West Angeles Church of God in Christ, First A.M.E.,

> if indeed we are one in christ, we the people of christ should be able to overcome the divisiveness that sometimes springs from our differences.

and the Crenshaw Christian Center. I am aware of several other churches with at least one thousand members in southern California. The resistance is being overcome with some success. Still, we cannot deny that many small and struggling churches are in need of help in this present socio-political climate of apathy and often hostility.

BUILDING ON OUR Differences

The differences in our worlds are often underscored by polls, media, politics, and the social sciences. Some of our observations of these differences may have validity, while others are subjective and unconvincing. Nonetheless, the church planter's concern is not to engage in useless debates about our biases. A more significant purpose would be to understand the peculiarities of the people being served and to capitalize on those peculiarities.

The church planter must recognize that differences are just that. Judgment must be suspended. The primary questions must be, What are the needs of these people and how can the church best meet those needs? The church planter has to know his audience if he is to institute successful and relevant ministries in their context. Even though various vehicles are used to highlight our differences in controversial ways, we may utilize a consciousness of our cultural heritage in a beneficial manner.

> SOCIAL ENGAGEMENT IS A NECESSARY COMPONENT OF BEING CONTEXTUALLY RELEVANT. BY SOCIAL ENGAGEMENT I MEAN THAT ONE MUST BE INTIMATELY INVOLVED WITH THE MEMBERS OF THE TARGET GROUP.

The African-American church planter must have a clear concept of contextual relevancy as it pertains to his field of ministry. A contextually relevant church planter is one who is proficient in the recognition and application of the salient underpinnings of his target group. For example, it is important to know what the target group's social structures are, how it solves problems, what its history is, what its expectations of leadership are, what the educational level of its members is, and other such factors. Obviously, the more data that can be collected on the target group, the more successful the church planter will be in developing a relevant ministry to the group. Confusion occurs when the church planter is inept in terms of discerning the peculiar nuances of the target group.

summary

Unfortunately, if the African-American church planter fails to understand the importance of contextual relevancy, considerable frustration will result from his attempt to establish a church. Simply because a person lives within a geographical area does not necessarily insure a proficient working knowledge of the social imperatives of the people in that area. This applies even if the church planter is of the same ethnic group as they are.

Social engagement is a necessary component of being contextually relevant. By social engagement I mean that one must be intimately involved with the members of the target group, having a thoroughgoing knowledge of them and their ways so that it becomes evident that he is one of them. It is through such affiliation that the church planter may effectively orchestrate a viable plant. A good grasp of the social norms of the target group is most essential for an effective church plant to occur.

Chapter Two

HOW african-american churches are planted

> Conflict is the gadfly of thought. It stirs us to observation and memory. It instigates invention. It shocks us out of sheep-like passivity, and sets us at noting and contriving.... conflict is a "sine qua non" of reflection and ingenuity.
>
> —John Dewey

seeking a better motive

Calvary Baptist Church of Santa Ana had gone through several years of conflict with their pastor because of philosophical differences. Pastor Davidson's approach to ministry was considered too domineering and liberal. A power struggle ensued between the pastor and the official board. Eventually the Rev. Mr. Davidson was asked to vacate his office, but he refused to do so. He maintained that the order for him to vacate was unlawful and in violation of both the church's constitution and his contract of employment. The matter was decided in the court and the ruling went against the pastor. Evidently the ordeal took a toll on his marriage, which ended in divorce. Mr.

Davidson was expelled from the church and took approximately fifty loyal members with him to plant a church in Inglewood, California.

The next pastor of Calvary Baptist, the Rev. Mr. Franklin, remained there for four years and was also expelled, being charged with marital infidelity. He took about a hundred loyal members with him and planted a church in the Culver City area. So within ten years, Calvary Baptist had two church splits that unintentionally resulted in two churches being planted. In both instances a plant was made possible only because of conflict and discord.

Far too often churches are planted out of discontent and splitting in an unorthodox manner. When a new church begins this way, it already has several strikes against it. First, the motivation for starting the church is usually wrong. Disagreement among people in a given body is not necessarily a valid reason for some of the people to leave and attempt to build a new church. Second, the support of a mother church, which can lend needed assistance in the early stages of the new plant, is usually absent. It is unfortunate that there aren't some guidelines to govern church planting in the independent African-American churches. As a result, members with little or no ability for the task have often gone out attempting to establish churches. Furthermore, it is often the case that too little planning has been given to the most adequate location to begin a church plant. I can point to several areas in Los Angeles where at least three small churches exist on the same block. Some of these congregations are of the same denomination. The frustration that results from church splits

> IT IS UNFORTUNATE THAT THERE AREN'T SOME GUIDELINES TO GOVERN CHURCH PLANTING IN THE INDEPENDENT AFRICAN-AMERICAN CHURCHES.

and unprepared pastors virtually rushing into the pastorate does not permit the kind of planning and forethought needed for sound church planting.

tHe caLL to pLantInG

The motivation for planting a new church should be considered with extreme carefulness. A number of factors must be pondered, not the least of which is whether a call to church planting is evident.

Recently I have seen several churches begin and then fail in short order. My observation was that none of the planting pastors appeared to possess the relational skills or the aptitude for pastoral work. Evidently some think that just anyone can start a church and see it flourish. Clearly, contemporary church planting calls for a relatively high degree of skill and commitment. One sure indicator of one's call is the ability to continue even in the face of insurmountable odds. If a true call is not there, the severe demands of church planting will probably ferret out the impostor.

Some pastors apparently plant churches because they are unable to secure a desirable appointment otherwise. It may be a lack of pastoral ethics and demeanor that keeps such persons frustrated. Still others do not have the training, experience, or education that is required to obtain an appointment. Some have qualifications but have no connections or allies who can assist them in getting appointed, and they lack the ability to achieve it alone. Any of these kinds of frustrations can become an undesirable motivation for planting a church. When a certain godly call is absent as a motivating factor in church planting, God's blessing will not likely be on such a venture. Spiritual failure will most certainly be assured. Unless the planting pastor is unusually talented and determined, he will often abandon the effort, causing many who have followed him to be discouraged and confused.

Obviously there are exceptions. Some have gone on to make exceptional strides in terms of building edifices and attracting huge numbers of people. Yet the fruit of their work often indicates a lack of devotion to the Lord. The demands of the pastorate today are staggering. Therefore, it is incumbent upon every church planter to ascertain whether he has received a true call prior to beginning a church plant.

In a survey of African-American pastors in which about fifteen responded, only one said that his motivation for beginning a church plant was to help a group after a church split. The others reported that they felt that the Lord was leading them to plant a church. One of these also indicated that he was frustrated where he was in his ministry. Prior to the survey done in the winter of 1995, I had spoken to a good number of pastors who casually admitted to starting churches simply out of a desire to pastor a church. I believe that we must give some serious attention to our motivation for church-planting ventures. Several things appear to be imperative regarding a call to church planting. Let us look at some of them.

A sincere desire to reach a given target group with the gospel message and to disciple that group is of utmost importance in church planting. The emphasis is not on the servant but on the quality of the service. In order to reach a given community, we must have an appreciation for its demographics. This will enable the church to design an approach to ministry that is contextually relevant. Recognition of the education, employment, recreation, and other socio-economic indicators will help the church planter in the effective development of a ministry plan. Obviously, when more is known about the target group, better planning can be done. Presumably, a genuine call will motivate the planter to learn about the community of people under consideration.

I must acknowledge that in the past many black churches were planted by men with little regard for demographics, formal education, extensive research, and long-term planning. Many of these churches were quite successful and still serve their communities today. Nonetheless, the contemporary church planter must recognize that many conventional and traditional models will not carry over into the twenty-first century. For example, in the past many African-Americans had a tradition of going to church, even if they were not believers. Now people tend to demand more from their church affiliation. They expect more from the ministry, and many also want to have more participation in the affairs of the church. Often the affairs of the church have been attended to by a strong pastor and/or a few key laypersons. Alternative forms of leadership and government may be expected for maximum progress in the coming years.

> a sincere desire to reach a given target group with the gospel message and to disciple that group is of utmost importance in church planting. the emphasis is not on the servant but on the quality of the service.

preparing to plant

When I began a church plant seven years ago in Inglewood, California, I soon discovered the importance of preparing for it. Being prepared may suggest a number of things. However, two of the most important technical activities one can do is to attend seminars and classes and to read everything that is being done in contemporary church planting. A good seminary education will certainly be essential, but it is not enough if one has not learned specifics about church planting. Proper training will allow the church planter to develop his own philosophy of ministry. It is also extremely beneficial for a prospective church planter to assist in the planting phase of a church as an apprentice under the leadership of a more experienced pastor. This is most important! I had occasion to work with Pastor Bill Burwell for one year prior to beginning a church plant. This experience allowed me to witness some of the practical aspects of this work. However, I had no formal training in specific matters to guide me in church planting.

I assumed, like many, that I could simply mimic other pastors, and everything would somehow just fall into place. Needless to say, I made many mistakes that could have been avoided if I had prepared properly. Of course, no amount of preparation will insure that every eventuality will be anticipated. Also, no amount of preparation can prevent the church planter from making some mistakes. However, many errors can be avoided with proper foresight. The progress of the ministry can be seriously hampered by proceeding in haphazard and inefficient ways. Contemporary church planters must accept the fact that we are living in an era that is significantly different from that of our fathers' generation.

In addition to the more technical aspects of church planting, the church planter must be prepared to deal with an array of attitudes as he attempts to forge a group of strangers into a unit. Church planting lends itself to a wide range of emotions. The roller-coaster effect becomes evident as the body of believers experiences success and failure in the ministry of its leaders. In my first two years at Emmaus Baptist, one of my most frustrating duties was trying to mediate between antagonists. Besides this, people became upset about not being recognized for their contributions, not receiving enough attention from the pastor, not getting enough church support for their projects, experiencing personality conflicts, and more. As I look back on those years, I can see that strangers were attempting to find their place and testing the level of commitment that the other believers had to one another. Many people have left the church or gone on to other churches. Yet many have remained and learned to work together for the common good. I was not really prepared for the stress of conflict resolution. The church planter will do well to learn some principles of and techniques for conflict resolution.

LoGistics of church plantinG

Logistically, one must be prepared to deal with the lack of adequate worship and administrative facilities. The absence of these can be a definite impediment to the ministry's progress. The first place where Emmaus Baptist met was at a hotel. A high level of noise and other disruptive elements were detrimental to developing an atmosphere for worship. Often churches in the urban context begin in storefronts and may be displaced several times within a short span. These less-than-desirable quarters coupled with frequent moves give the congregation an impression of instability. In practically every move some members drop out because of distance or disillusionment or for other reasons. This is a difficult problem for urban planters, and it may require some new strategies for them to overcome it. One possibility is to contract with an existing church to meet in their facilities during their off hours. This will allow for a setting that may be more conducive to worship. I have found that many urbanites do not feel good about going to places of worship that are not expressly designed for worship.

I contracted with an Anglo-Presbyterian church after a couple of inadequate meeting places did not work out. The availability of "church" facilities immediately elevated the congregation's morale. One could argue that it should not make any difference where we meet, as long as we have the Spirit of the Lord with us. While this is true in theory, as a practical matter it does not necessarily follow. Many churches are willing to contract to share their facilities with another body, especially if it is of a different ethnic and denominational orientation. When the host church is attempting to reach the same target group as the newcomers, it will be less likely to be willing to share its facilities with them. Therefore, a black church will not be quick to share its facilities with another black church on a long-term basis. Conversely, several African-American churches are now sharing their buildings with Latino ministries. One of the most efficient ways of getting started is to share space with a host church that is already established.

As a matter of caution, I must say that people need to be motivated to become emancipated and independent. Initially, a goal should be set as to how long the church plans to be a guest church. My experience has been that often the guest congregation becomes very much satisfied with the arrangement and has little motivation for contributing to a building fund. If building is an important aspect of the new church's plan and philosophy, this concern must be anticipated and encouraged. Otherwise the church may settle for guest status for an indeterminate period.

EVANGELISM AND CHURCH PLANTING

Finally, one must consider an effective outreach methodology prior to planting a church. The church's philosophy regarding evangelism and discipleship is a key element in its eventual prosperity. The absence of a plan for reaching the target group with the gospel message and of the ability to assimilate them into the church will virtually assure failure in a church plant.

One of the greatest frustrations is in assimilating new people into the church if the church has not been trained in methods of assimilation. Fewer people are walking through the front door cold off the streets today. We must devise means of getting them into the body of believers and keeping them there. No longer can we simply build a church and expect that people will automatically come to it. We must decide to build new churches by reaching new believers, not by transfer memberships. One of the problems of church-split start-ups is that of depending on disgruntled people who may have little commitment to the church. Such a beginning will often lead to lethargy or outright failure if not properly understood. Indeed, Robert E. Logan recognized this effect when he said,

> an effective contextually relevant approach to outreach will enable the new church to focus primarily on new converts in order to achieve growth. the Great commission will be fulfilled as well.

> Too many churches pad their rolls with the Christians who shuffle from church to church. Ironically, while attracting disgruntled Christians presents a tempting way to boost growth initially, it is often because of the sort of person who is unwilling to commit his loyalty to a church that these churches begin to decay.[2]

The contemporary church planter must avoid the common temptation of using "church hoppers" as a primary basis for church growth. An effective contextually relevant approach to outreach will enable the new church to focus primarily on new converts in order to achieve growth. The Great Commission will be fulfilled as well (Matt. 28:19–20).

When Emmaus Baptist was planted, our primary means of evangelism was confrontational. That is, we canvassed the neighborhood and attempted to meet strangers and to share the gospel with them. We had a measurable degree of success with reaching some people with the gospel message, but we were terribly ineffective in terms of assimilating them into the body. It was like giving birth and leaving the baby on the doorstep. Needless to say, this was most frustrating. We still do some door-to-door outreach on occasion but are doing more to develop friendship methods of evangelism. Relationships are being forged on the job, in the family, and in the neighborhood. We are presently instituting small-group ministries in an effort to prepare the body to reach out in a less threatening and more meaningful manner. We have discovered that a quality system of assimilation is most imperative for developing a ministry.

errors in church planting

Charles Ridley suggested that there are five common errors made in selecting a church planter. He indicated that the following errors tend to hinder good decision making as it relates to such selection.

1. Not looking at enough candidates

Someone recently told me that his denomination has more new church planter positions than available people to fill the jobs. Therefore the denomination hires practically anyone who shows strong interest. This is one among many reasons why so few candidates are actually considered. It is an established fact in personnel work that the best selection decisions are made when there is a 4:1 or 5:1 ratio. For every position under consideration, there should be four or five candidates.

2. An inadequate position description

Some church planters do not understand what is expected of them. Denominational leaders themselves often are unclear about what they expect. This poses a tremendous problem. New church planters, eager and enthusiastic about their ministry, discover that the expectations and demands of the job are different from their own idealized expectations. This could lead to frustration, dissatisfaction, anger, and early resignation from the ministry.

3. Incomplete investigation procedures

Once a person becomes a candidate, there needs to be a complete investigation of the person's background. Otherwise, you run the risk of selecting someone with undesirable qualities.

4. Ineffective interviewing techniques

Interviewing is the most widely used method of making selection decisions. However, interviews are typically unreliable predictors of later performance. There are several major reasons for the unreliability of interviews. Interview content is rarely matched to the actual performance criteria of the job. Interviewer biases and stereotypes have significant impact on decision making. Also, interviewers are more influenced by negative information than by positive information.

5. Lack of clear criteria for selection

Until recently, no systematic attempt to identify the criteria for effective church planters has been made. For this reason, most selection decisions in the past have been made on the basis of incomplete information. Researchers such as the Charles E. Fuller Institute have provided a clearer picture of what it takes to be a church planter.[3]

If we are going to avoid some of the mistakes of the past in selecting church planters, we must use the best available information. Contemporary church planting demands a more reasoned approach.

summary

A more concerted effort on the part of African-American church planters to establish churches in an intentional and planned manner is imperative. Today formal training and preparation are most essential for church-planting enterprises. When a pastor feels the call to plant a church, he will do well to get wise counsel, develop support, organize a strong core group, and be fully appraised of the community before planting a new church. Finally, a love for the community and a desire to reach it with the message of hope must be the primary motivations for ministry.

> a love for the community and a desire to reach it with the message of hope must be the primary motivations for ministry.

Chapter Three

WHY AFRICAN-AMERICAN CHURCHES ARE DIFFERENT FROM ANGLO CHURCHES

Though I am free and belong to no man, I make myself a slave to everyone, to win as many as possible. To the Jews I became like a Jew, to win the Jews. To those under the law I became like one under the law (though I myself am not under the law), so as to win those under the law.

—1 Corinthians 9:19–20

HISTORICAL REASONS FOR DIFFERENCES

If black and white Americans come from different worlds, we may expect them to have churches that are different. This may sound disturbing since there is only one true church and all believers are charged with being unified in Christ (Eph. 4:4). However, the difference that I speak of is one of degree rather than of kind. My assertion is that there can be valid variations within the body of Christ in areas where freedom is allowed.

In matters where the Scripture does not dictate conduct and behavior, we can and ought to allow differences of expression. This may account for differences in our respective churches, differences that are not a cause for alarm. For example, the Bible indicates that we may differ in dietary or holiday observances without passing judgment on one another (Rom. 14). Although there may be variants whose validity we could debate, by and large our diversity is due to differences in our history, socialization, and culture. The history of black and white America has been one that to a large degree was built on mistrust, servitude, and hate. Therefore a primary cause for denouncing differences in our respective churches may be one of perception regarding the relative value of the black church to make any meaningful contributions to the church at large.

We must level the barriers that have been erected between us before we can realize any genuine reconciliation. I can still remember traveling as a boy and not being able to use the facilities at gas stations or to get food except take-out, and then at the rear of the restaurant. Even when we are willing and desire to put these matters behind us, there is a history that has been set in motion. It takes an inordinate amount of time for the remnants of this kind of injustice to be fully eradicated. There are still those, both black and white, who find occasion to persist in perpetuating the old system.

Therefore it is the responsibility of conscientious and progressive people, especially Christians, to lead the charge in racial reconciliation. In order to do so, we must first destroy some of the myths associated with black people and white people. The most important one is that blacks are inherently inferior to whites. In his book *Let's Get to Know Each Other* Tony Evans explains,

> Myths are traditions passed down over time in story form as a means of explaining or justifying events that are lacking in either scientific evidence or historical basis.... Myths often have strong religious tenets associated with them.... Myths are powerful because they are believed and therefore become the basis of our actions as individuals, as families, and as a society at large.[1]

Since myths become embedded in society and take on the status of valid tradition, they are most difficult to overcome. For example, many believe that blacks are naturally inferior to whites intellectually. Still others maintain mythical notions regarding black sexuality, criminal behavior, spiritual maturity, and the like. Actually, we all have many successes and failures in all of these categories. The basis of our differences is established in history and sustained by social and cultural underpinnings.

From a purely sociological or psychological point of view, we may conclude that many people have sustained irreparable damage because of our common history. Some significant strides have been made by some social-awareness programs to overcome these damages. Yet the resources of such programs are very limited and results are generally superficial. Relationships that cannot undergo scrutiny or honesty of expression are the kind of shallow relationships that exist between the races.

An example of this is seen in how politically correct we must be in our words and deeds. Often our fragile relationships will not endure frankness, and a façade is all that we can tolerate. In Los Angeles we have seen how differences still are manifested, for example, during the recent court trials of Rodney King and O. J. Simpson. The reaction of people to the verdicts in these trials is itself an extraordinary case study in attitudinal differences in black and white America. I do not think that anyone can tell how long it takes to repair such deep-seated emotional wounds as we have sustained in our country. Even so, we the church have a responsibility to seek effective means of reconciling the people of God without respect to race, color, or historical considerations (see 2 Cor. 5:19–20).

SOCIAL THEORIES FOR DIFFERENCES

Social scientists have attempted to discern the cause of observable differences in the African-American church. C. Eric Lincoln, a social scientist at Duke University, related several theories in the book *The Black Church in the African-American Experience*. Like most theories, these offer some truth, but they are not conclusive. However, those who propound these theories recognize and accept the fact that significant differences do exist in the ways that many black and white churches conduct business. Lincoln indicated that the religious dimension of black churches is found in the black sacred cosmos, a unique Afro-Christian worldview that was forged among black people from both the African and Euro-American traditions during the eighteenth and nineteenth centuries. The black sacred cosmos permeated all of the social institutions and cultural traditions of black people. While the general structure of beliefs, rituals, and organization of black churches remained the same as white churches, black Christians often gave different nuances and

> RELATIONSHIPS THAT CANNOT UNDERGO SCRUTINY OR HONESTY OF EXPRESSION ARE THE KIND OF SHALLOW RELATIONSHIPS THAT EXIST BETWEEN THE RACES.... often OUR fragile RELATIONSHIPS WILL NOT ENDURE frankness, AND a façade IS ALL THAT WE CAN tolerate.

emphases to their theological views. For example, the paladin God of deliverance is given a much more prominent role in black worship practices. Black worship and religious experiences are also much more ecstatic, emotionally expressive, and enthusiastic compared to whites. The black sacred cosmos also reflects the deepest values of African Americans, giving primal consideration to the necessity of freedom as an expression of complete belonging and allegiance to God.[2]

These observations appear to be valid in general and are built upon a tradition that was based on the unique circumstances of Africans coming to America. Cultural norms and traditions are most difficult to dissociate oneself from, especially when one is dependent on them for a link to one's identity.

Again, from a scientific viewpoint, theories have been advanced in an attempt to explain the differences observed between black and white churches. Here I will summarize five of the most salient models.

The Assimilation Model

The assimilation model essentially teaches that the demise of the black church is necessary for the public good of blacks. According to this view, the black church is an impediment to the assimilation of African-Americans into the mainstream of American society. Those who hold this view claim that the black church is anti-intellectual and authoritarian. The model has been advanced by E. Franklin Frazier.

The Isolation Model

The isolation model claims that due to its predominantly lower-class station the black community is characterized as being involuntarily isolated. This is said to be evident in the resultant ghetto segregation, supported by mass apathy and isolation from civic affairs. Consequently, black religion is viewed as being of a lower status and otherworldly. The writings of Anthony Orum and Charles Silberman advance such notions.

The Compensatory Model

According to the compensatory model, the black church exists as an opportunity to empower the masses for esteem, applause, and control among its people. Supposedly, this is necessary because such opportunity is not afforded in the larger society. Authors Horace Cayton and St. Clair Drake espoused this view in their book *Black Metropolis*. Basically, this model concludes that black society is pathological and has a twisted view of American culture. Therefore there is a need for the development of its own institutions.

> ACCORDING TO THE COMPENSATORY MODEL, THE BLACK CHURCH EXISTS AS AN OPPORTUNITY TO EMPOWER THE MASSES FOR ESTEEM, APPLAUSE, AND CONTROL AMONG ITS PEOPLE.

The Ethnic Community-Prophetic Model

In their work *Black Church in the Sixties,* Hart and Anne Nelsen identified the models reported thus far. Furthermore, they developed the "ethnic community-prophetic" model, which apparently gives a more positive spin on the black church. Their model alludes to the significance of the black church "as a base for building a sense of ethnic identity and a community of interest among its members." They also emphasize the potential of the church as a "prophet to a corrupt white Christian nation."[3]

The Dialectical Model

Finally, C. Eric Lincoln advances the dialectical model of the black church. He sees the black church as being involved in a perpetual polarized dialectic. In his system, the church is the arbiter of certain tensions that are constantly shifting, depending on the exigencies of the time. The most prominent dialectics are between priestly and prophetic functions, universalism and particularism, privatistic and communal, charismatic and bureaucratic, otherworldly and this-worldly, and between resistance and accommodation. The complexity of the church is indicated by the vast continuum that it operates along. The dialectical model attempts to take into account the dynamics and complexities of the black church in a more comprehensive way.

summary

A major shortcoming of the models other than the dialectical is that they tend to be rather reductionistic in their view and understanding of the institution under discussion. Such simplified approaches allow for a continuation of myths about the black church. For example, although assimilation may be desirable, it does not necessarily follow that all of the cultural imperatives of any ethnic group must cease in order to obtain an acceptable measure of assimilation. Further, these models tend to portray differences in terms of inferiority, without fully examining the context in which they exist.

The black church is different from the white church as a practical matter because we have had different orientations historically. Lincoln's model is built on W. E. B. DuBois's "phenomenology of consciousness." DuBois's notion was that African-Americans possess a double consciousness as summarizing both the plight and the potential of the African and the

Euro-American heritage: "two struggling souls within one dark body."[4] Lincoln concludes that his model leads to a more dynamic view of black churches along a continuum of dialectical tensions, struggles, and changes. Moreover, the problem that he sees with the single nondialectical topological views of black churches is that they tend to classify and stereotype black churches into rigid pigeonhole categories, such as "other-worldly." Their inflexibility misses the historical dynamism of institutions moving back and forth because of certain issues or social conditions.[5]

Chapter Four

Leadership in african - american churches

The more voices we allow to speak about one thing, the more eyes, different eyes we can use to observe one thing, the more complete will our concept of this thing, our objectivity, be.

—Friedrich Nietzsche

traditional roles of leadership

As I have suggested, some think of leadership in the African-American church as being authoritarian and misguided at best. Traditionally, the minister was one of a few professionals in the black community and was very highly respected and looked to for guidance in many areas of life. The black minister was not simply a spiritual leader. He was also a politician, civil-rights advocate, bail bondsman, teacher, fund-raiser, and more. The leader of the black church was socially engaged and arguably enmeshed in the social affairs of the community to an unhealthy degree.

The relatively slender basis of professionals in earlier times caused the community to depend heavily on teachers, preachers, and morticians for professional assistance. Often these professionals were one and the same. The context in which African-American society developed did not encourage and in some cases did not allow for widespread professional development in the black community. Therefore those few persons who had acquired formal education were depended on in an absolute and inordinate manner.

I can remember that in my youth a number of men were teacher, preacher, notary public, and generally the community service liaison regarding professional matters. The contemporary church planter must understand the expectations of his target group. Only then can he properly assess what can be tolerated as acceptable and what must be renegotiated in view of the times. Another concern of today's church planter is a consideration of what is a biblical model as opposed to the traditional model. He must raise the question, What is my godly role as a leader in the church today?

In an attempt to be contextually relevant, the church planter must appreciate the historical factors that shaped the present expectations. The black church historian Carter G. Woodson offered some insight into the inclusive role of the early black church in America:

> The Negro church as a social force in the life of the race is nothing new. Prior to emancipation the church was the only institution which, in a few places in the South and throughout the North, the Negro was permitted to maintain for his own peculiar needs. Offering the only avenue for the expressional activities of the race, the church answered many a social purpose for which this institution among other groups differently circumstanced had never before been required to serve.[1]

The contemporary church planter, as pastor, is well advised to avoid trying to do all that may be demanded of him. Instead, he must instruct others and learn to delegate authority when appropriate. Indeed, any church planter would do well to recall the apostle's declaration when he said, "So neither he who plants nor he who waters is anything, but only God, who makes things grow... For we are God's fellow workers; you are God's field, God's building" (1 Cor. 3:7, 9).

Moreover, the contemporary church planter must not allow tradition to supplant his God-given call to equip the saints for Christian service (Eph. 4:12). The demand on the African-American pastor is exacerbated by the peculiar circumstances that beset the masses. Yet he must maintain a balance between the social, political, and spiritual dimensions of the culture in which the church exists. At the same instance, he must be able to properly integrate these factors.

We need to applaud churches that address the felt needs of people and are feeding, clothing, housing, and training people for employment. Some of the prominent churches have a keen sense of reaching people by ministering to their social and economic needs. Undoubtedly, this is why they thrive in proximity to other churches that are struggling. Even so, the black church is cautioned not to lose sight of the fact that people have a spiritual hunger and thirst that is as compelling as their physical ones. My observation is that several leaders in the Los Angeles area have very efficient outreach programs, but the content of the biblical message preached is decidedly shallow. Admittedly, there are many churches in the community that are preaching excellent biblical messages to the church and at the same time have little or no vision for reaching the lost. My contention is that we must develop the

> my contention is that we must develop the ministry in a holistic way, maintaining a harmony between its spiritual and social aspects.

ministry in a holistic way, maintaining a harmony between its spiritual and social aspects.

new models of Leadership

The leadership model that Jesus used certainly included reaching people where they were. It meant ministering to their total needs. We can recall the biblical account of Jesus feeding the five thousand:

> When Jesus looked up and saw a great crowd coming toward him, he said to Philip, "Where shall we buy bread for these people to eat?"... After the people saw the miraculous sign that Jesus did, they began to say, "Surely this is the Prophet who is to come into the world."
>
> John 6:5, 14

Obviously, Jesus was concerned about the physical welfare of these people and did something about it. He fed them. However, there is a clear indication that He was ministering in a way that was spiritually enlightening. The people recognized that He was the One to come, apparently a reference to the Messiah. In addition, Jesus was teaching His disciples some valuable lessons by His model. Ostensibly, as Jesus took the disciples along as He ministered, He was in fact training them to do what He did. The leadership model that we adopt in contemporary church planting must become an increasingly shared or team effort.

Traditionally, the demands on leadership in the black church have been rather generalized and comprehensive. The expectations of leadership were based on the needs of the community. Today, with an expanding base of professional and educated people in the body, more ministry can be done by the people. Church growth will be enhanced by unleashing the congregation for ministry.

A signal difference in emphasis between the black and the white churches in America has been a significant focus on social and political matters in the black church. Without further examination of the cause, it would be a mistake to assume that this represents an inferior approach to ministry. In addition, we may be able to make similar parallels in the prevailing situations in other areas. In earlier years, the leader in the black church had a constituency that required and demanded eventual relief in terms of social and political concerns. This was primarily because blacks had been systematically denied access to such arenas. The church was the only reliable institution that the African-American had for redressing his concerns in an effective way.

One can argue whether some of the tactics used were legitimate or even biblical. Clearly, the option to turn the other cheek and to wait patiently could be invoked when we examine the tactics of those who engaged in civil disobedience. Similarly, we can challenge the majority's position of acknowledging freedom in Christ while allowing the government to promote classism and racism without challenging the nation's conscience on the issues. There is a ton of blame to be placed on both black and white Christians, but that is not the point. The contemporary church planter must understand the demands on the ministry in light of history and a proper biblical model.

> TODAY, WITH AN EXPANDING BASE of PROFESSIONAL AND EDUCATED PEOPLE IN THE BODY, MORE MINISTRY CAN BE DONE BY THE PEOPLE. CHURCH GROWTH WILL BE ENHANCED BY UNLEASHING THE CONGREGATION FOR MINISTRY.

Today's church planter must be highly trained and have a vivid perception of his target group. In addition, he must be adept in administering the practical along with the theoretical.

This is why I feel strongly that church planting has to be contextually relevant. Again, this requires a curriculum in our seminaries and Bible schools that is sensitive to the cultural considerations of various groups. Surely, much of the information garnered from our institutions can be applied to any situation. It is universal. Even so, perhaps 10 to 15 percent of the contents may need context-specific treatment. This is especially true for leaders working in highly homogeneous groups that are not Anglo. Much of the material written on contemporary church planting has been done by white authors and is primarily geared to white audiences. This is to be expected. That is the reason why African-American leaders and other minorities must become more productive in terms of publishing contextually relevant literature. If indeed there are significant differences, each group must bear the primary burden of laboring in its own field.

Ranjit DeSilva did a study of some prominent black churches in Los Angeles to get a bearing on charismatic leaders in the community. He concluded his study by saying,

> Some African American charismatic leaders I interviewed were self-taught and had not been through formal Bible or theological education. They usually have not fitted into the school system and learned to think in that mold. They have approached ministry differently and yet have had success. One leader indicated that traditional seminary deals with the theoretical, not with the practical. . . . Another leader said that the very nature of the "charisma"—grace from God—implies that it is a gift from above.[2]

Clearly, there are some charismatic personalities in all communities that can amass significant ministries without reliance on formal constructs. The African-American church has a number of such leaders. Nevertheless, even these ministers could improve their skills and sharpen their gifts by being more informed.

evidence of new directions

There are some strong and growing churches in the urban centers, and there is some evidence among them of new directions. Some leaders are accepting the challenge to develop intentional church-planting churches. Ratcliff and Cox report regarding the situation then and now:

> My research uncovered what I believe is the greatest untold church-planting story of the twentieth century. In 1900 there were a few black churches in Northern industrial cities. Today there are thousands. This growth has mainly taken place without planning, without outside support, and without human supervision. It was done with great sacrifice by church-planter pastors who made their own living.[3]

Here Ratcliff and Cox give an account of how leaders have traditionally planted churches in the black community. Unfortunately, most are still planted in this way. Yet there is some progress to report. They observe,

> However, that paradigm is now shifting. Church planting in black communities is becoming more intentional. Strong black churches are deliberately, under the Holy Spirit's leadership, training and sending out church planters. Pastors of predominantly black churches are supervising these church planters. Monetary support is coming from these sponsoring churches.[4]

Surely, it is this kind of new vision and corporate effort that will be necessary for church planting in the future. This is encouraging. Still, unfortunately, many black churches continue to be planted in the traditional way—church splitting, tension, and little planning. In order to establish more strong churches with a vision for church planting, contemporary leaders must assume responsibility for creating an atmosphere where this is possible.

There are other encouraging signs of potential for progress in African-American churches. For example, Leith Anderson reports, "Nationally, African American churches are increasing at the rate of 13.5% annually."[5] Clearly, this is a significant rate of growth, which can be improved only with careful planning and vision.

Those who work in urban America must also realize that many churches will never grow beyond a modest group. Even though by contemporary standards these churches may never be successful, they may be used to reach enclaves of spiritually and economically disenfranchised people. Some of these churches are in the ghettos and housing projects. They may never become self-supporting. In such cases, it takes a special commitment to ministry to reach everyone with the gospel message.

IN ORDER TO ESTABLISH MORE STRONG CHURCHES WITH A VISION FOR CHURCH PLANTING, CONTEMPORARY LEADERS MUST ASSUME RESPONSIBILITY FOR CREATING AN ATMOSPHERE WHERE THIS IS POSSIBLE.

Again, the burden of the black pastor is the immense expectation people have of him. The dearth of human and economic resources weighs heavily on the pastor who wants earnestly to do all that his ministry demands. Gregory Reed speaks to the wide span of the ministry, declaring,

Wholistic is a word mentioned frequently today whenever the ministry and mission of the black church are discussed. What it means is that the black church has begun to re-focus its attention on the critical needs of the whole individual and the whole community rather than on just spiritual or religious needs.[6]

In view of the breadth and depth of the black pastor's ministry, it is incumbent upon him to devise efficient means of conducting ministry.

summary

Contemporary leadership in the urban context must focus keenly on a revised theology, philosophy, and strategy for church planting and growth in the black community. This is necessary because of a widespread lack of intentional church planting in the past. Furthermore, consideration must be given to the inordinate number of unchurched African-Americans and the lack of published resources on this subject. The demands of the urban community are quite formidable.

ministry in african-american churches

> Therefore, since through God's mercy we have this ministry, we do not lose heart.
>
> —2 Corinthians 4:1

traditional ministry emphases

In a large measure, ministry in many black churches has been conducted on a programmatic model. Many events on the church's calendar revolve around programs that are often perpetuated from one year to the next, each event taking place at the same time of year.

While this has been efficient in terms of planning and preparation, it may stifle creativity. Also, the doldrums may set in because the congregation knows essentially what to expect in advance. Of course, programs can provide a lot of activity in the church, but the contemporary church planter must ask if current programs are going to meet the needs of the church adequately. This is especially true regarding spiritual life in the body. Often programs that lend themselves to more social and cultural aspects of ministry are the more well received. These programs are certainly important, but when the spiritual disciplines (prayer, fasting, teaching, reaching, etc.) are shallow, then the church is required to question its approach to ministry. Events like men's day, women's day, and ushers' day virtually fill the calendar in some communities.

> MANY EVENTS ON THE CHURCH'S CALENDAR REVOLVE AROUND PROGRAMS THAT ARE OFTEN PERPETUATED FROM ONE YEAR TO THE NEXT. . . . WHILE THIS HAS BEEN EFFICIENT IN TERMS OF PLANNING AND PREPARATION, IT MAY STIFLE CREATIVITY.

Apparently, one of the key reasons that the programmatic model of ministry has been implemented is financial. A significant amount of money can be raised from programs during the course of a year. Therefore it is quite tempting to develop such an approach. What is the alternative to a purely programmatic approach? If the congregant can be effectively discipled regarding giving, a major advance will have been realized. Gregory J. Reed believes that

> God nowhere in His Word says that His Churches are to have sales, raffles, or bazaars to raise money for their work. God does not want His children to be beggars, going out in the world asking for means to carry on. . . . God only gives one plan of church finance in the Bible, and that is TITHES and OFFERINGS from His people.[1]

Therefore there is the need to gradually overcome simple tradition, which has become a mainstay in many congregations and therefore an expectation. That is, people expect certain familiar systems to persist, unless they can be convinced that a change is in order.

The main reason that many programs must be replaced in the contemporary black church is that much of ministry has revolved around concerns that have little or no bearing on the spiritual development of the saints or on reaching the lost. Rather, much of ministry involves socials and fund-raisers.

These aspects of ministry are important. Still, unless they are in balance with a strong teaching, discipleship, and evangelistic emphasis, the church will never reach its potential. A vast number of unbelievers exist within the urban context, and they will not be reached by introspective efforts like teas, banquets, yard sales, barbecues, or special annual days. Although there are many notable exceptions, still far too many black churches are operating on a model of ministry that is arguably outdated.

CONTEMPORARY MINISTRY APPROACHES

At this point, the church planter must take a holistic approach to congregational affairs. The entire life of the congregation must be considered. We must no longer advance a compartmentalized approach, wherein people come to church on Sunday morning and forget about spiritual commitments afterward. We must use a method in which every aspect of life is considered spiritual. Small groups, when properly instituted, will enable the African-American church to move beyond the programmatic approach to ministry. When small groups are instituted, people will begin to discover more about one another and about the practical applications of biblical principles. All aspects of the believer's life must be seen as having a spiritual connection.

On balance, it is important to realize that many African-American churches do involve themselves in community outreach. This is especially true of urban churches. However, outreach must be characterized by an approach that is both social and spiritual. In a survey of 1,459 black churches, these churches were asked about their involvement in community outreach with nonchurch agencies and programs. Of the rural churches 25.6 percent answered affirmatively. Eric Lincoln, who conducted the survey, points out that there is a high incidence of involvement by black churches with nonchurch agencies, showing that black churches are not privatized and uninvolved as some have suggested. The point can also be made that the necessity for balance in the spiritual development of black congregations must be a priority.

Given that the African-American church has had to meet a wide diversity of needs, its ministry has developed in ways that are significantly different from those of some Anglo congregations. Since many blacks were discouraged from advancing in public life, the church became the key arena for recognition and affirmation. Again Lincoln reports,

> The daily functioning and internal life of black churches is carried on by a variety of people connected to the church besides the pastor. In examining how black churches are able to maintain themselves, we asked about their staffing needs and what kinds of groups and organizations are found within black churches.[2]

Moreover, St. Clair Drake and Horace Cayton in their classic work observe that

> the large, mixed type of black urban churches, and sometimes even smaller ones, generated a variety of subgroups in which lay members of similar social status, needs, and interests could interact with each other. Internal life of most black churches is defined by small groups and auxiliaries who perform much of the work of organizing, planning, and executing the events and activities which distinguish each local congregation.[3]

The church has served as a center of influence both socially and religiously, mainly because it has been the primary institution in black society.

So then, there is a real sense in which small groups have long since been instituted in African-American churches. Yet the scope and range of what can be accomplished in small groups must be understood. We must be aware of the need to organize small groups and to explore how they can be used to enhance the whole of the church's life and ministry. If the contemporary church is to reach the next generation, its ministry must be relevant and sensitive to the needs of its target group, and small groups can help to accomplish this. George Barna declared that

> PEOPLE MUST BE MADE TO RECOGNIZE THAT THE CHURCH IS A WAY OF LIFE. FAR TOO MANY SEE THE CHURCH AS BEING A SUNDAY-MORNING EXPERIENCE OF A COUPLE OF HOURS' DURATION.

> successful churches remain sensitive to the people they were seeking to reach and serve. This meant understanding how people in their community live, and what needs they have which a church might address. It also meant staying informed about how people respond to the church itself.[4]

If our ministry is not opened to evaluation and made to maintain relevancy, the progress of the church will be seriously hampered.

People must be made to recognize that the church is a way of life. Far too many see the church as being a Sunday-morning experience of a couple of hours' duration. Clearly, this is an erroneous view of the church. In the future, the difference between success and mediocrity in the church will be the ability of people to see Christianity as a lifestyle, rather than a Sunday-morning expression. In his studies Barna states,

> Individuals who became regulars at successful churches understood that real Christianity is not a spectator sport. It is a participatory, hands-on way of life. They were compelled by calling and desire, rather than ritualistic obligation, to play a role in the work of the church.[5]

It is disturbing to observe the number of persons who serve in the church and at the same time live openly carnal lifestyles. If the church is to operate with power and integrity, more people must be persuaded to embrace the living Christ and accept Christianity as a lifestyle.

REASONS FOR DIFFERENCES BETWEEN BLACK AND WHITE CHURCHES

There are significant differences in terms of ministry application between the black and white churches, and there are reasons for these differences. For example, previously many black ministers were not allowed access to certain seminaries and colleges. Therefore much of the traditional black religious expression has been oral and often self-generated. In general, the white tradition has been more academic and reduced to writing. Regarding finance, traditionally many blacks have not been privileged to enjoy the same levels of wealth or formal training in finance as whites have. Hence, many African-American churches have relied on common-sense approaches in ministry. However, it is important to note that some differences may not be as significant as they appear on face. For example, although black traditions and experiences have been developed differently, essentially they are in alignment with true biblical doctrine. Tony Evans has rightly observed,

... we cannot speak of Evangelicalism and exclude the black church, which has always held to historic Protestant Christian doctrine. In fact the church was founded and then flourished in a conservative biblical tradition.[6]

He went on to say,

Yet the broader evangelical community has not taken the black church seriously and has encouraged black Christians to do likewise because its theological expression has been oral tradition, rather than a literary tradition, that results in textbooks and formal theological statements.[7]

As new churches are planted in the black community, leadership must consider new models. Since assimilation, training, and more opportunities have become a reality, it is imperative that leaders take responsibility for progressive measures in ministry.

> at present, more black ministers are privileged to receive formal education than previously. consequently, it is incumbent upon them to write and become more involved in academia.

summary

At present, more black ministers are privileged to receive formal education than previously. Consequently, it is incumbent upon them to write and become more involved in academia. This will result in a better understanding between the races. It will also allow for a more informed assessment of affairs in the community, which all may benefit from. The best one to tell a story is the one whose story it is.

Chapter Six

contemporary preaching in african-american churches

One does not improve through argument but through examples....
Be what you wish to make others become. Make yourself, not your
words, a sermon.

—Henri-Frédéric Amiel

HOW BLACK PREACHING DEVELOPED

Preaching has been a major factor in the ministry of African-American churches since their inception. There appears to be little opposition to the belief in the validity of the Bible as the Word of God. Biblical authority has not been a major challenge for the black preacher. It has been relatively easy for him to express the truth of the Bible and to relate it to the black context.

The genius of black pastors to make the Bible relevant may account for the level of acceptance their messages enjoy. Blacks in America have identified with Israel as being a people who were displaced and despised. Furthermore, liberal theology has not been introduced into the mainstream black churches for the most part. Although the pulpit has been a platform for addressing many of society's ills, both social and spiritual, a strong emphasis has been placed on sound doctrine.

The contemporary pastor has to decide on the style and demeanor of his preaching ministry. Some people have suggested that "prophetic" black preaching is too emotional and even shallow. However, the context in which the preaching takes place must be considered before any strict conclusions are drawn. If preaching is to have contextual relevancy, it must address the audience under consideration.

> THE TRADITION OF BLACK PREACHING DEVELOPED IN A CONTEXT OF DIRE CIRCUMSTANCES. THE NEED TO ENGENDER A DEGREE OF HOPE IN A CLIMATE OF DESPAIR LED TO A PARTICULAR KIND OF PREACHING.

To best appreciate the experiences and needs of a people, one should have experiences similar to theirs. The tradition of black preaching developed in a context of dire circumstances. The need to engender a degree of hope in a climate of despair led to a particular kind of preaching. In addition, the cultural considerations of African people must be understood. This can be seen in their ecstasy in worship and in their oral tradition. Therefore differences must be seen not in terms of value judgments, but rather as cultural differences first. Only when a matter clearly goes against Scripture can we properly make negative value judgments.

The environment in which preaching is conducted must influence its style and content. The scriptural emphasis and the manner of its interpretation and application will be related to the situation. Regarding such relevancy, Henry H. Mitchell explained,

> Black preaching is conditioned by the sociology, eco-
> nomics, government, culture, the total ethos of the Black
> ghetto. It is also affected by (and producing and chang-
> ing) both a Black summa theological and, in particular, a
> theology about itself.[1]

I can still remember quite vividly having visited my home-
town of Monticello, Florida, about fourteen years ago. A two
days' preaching assignment was granted me by my home
church, Hickory Hill Missionary Baptist. I had been preaching
intermittently for a couple of years. Some family members and
old acquaintances were there for support and also out of curios-
ity, I'm sure. At the conclusion of my first message an elderly
deacon whom I knew got up and said, "Today he taught, maybe
tomorrow he will preach." I might add that I thought I had
preached. This experience left an indelible impression upon me
regarding what many black congregations expect of preaching.

The differences in preaching styles that one may observe in
many black congregations can be explained, in part, within a
historical framework. As I have indicated, many within the
black religious experience gave allegiance to biblical faith and
witness because their own experiences seemed to be depicted
in the Bible. Carl H. Felder offers this explanation for the historical biblical application in the African-American context:

> Since most of the earliest African American Christians had
> been denied, from the beginning of their experience in the
> Americas, the opportunity to be fully human, including the
> opportunity to learn to read and write, the "letters" of bib-
> lical texts were not crucial in their appropriation and redac-
> tion of Christian traditions. What became important was
> the telling and retelling, the hearing and the re-hearing of

biblical stories of perseverance, of strength in weakness and under oppressive burdens, of hope in hopeless situations.[2]

It is most important that the contemporary African-American church planters have an appreciation for the reasons that certain conditions exist within the context. Otherwise, an insensitivity to protocol can result in disaster.

A case in point is related by a friend whom I will call Pastor Willis, who planted a church in the Moreno Valley, California, area. He had support from his parent church and also at the denominational level. He had an able core group. Pastor Willis had been trained in and graduated from seminary. In a word, he had enough training, assistance, and support to have made extraordinary inroads in a growing unchurched community. Yet he failed miserably after a couple of struggling years. He now admits that his attempt to dismiss all traces of traditional black culture from the church's structure was a major cause of his failure. Pastor Willis wanted to dismiss and downplay any black cultural norms in songs, preaching, organizational structure, and the like.

The contemporary church planter must take time to determine what his congregation expects of him and decide what he is willing to do. If there is not a meeting of the minds, then a church plant should not be attempted.

The black church has enjoyed a distinguished degree of prominence in terms of the preaching ministry. From the 1700s to the present, numerous luminaries have graced pulpits in the black community. Some of them were prominent only in the black church. One only has to be reminded of Richard Allen, Andrew Bryan, J. W. C. Pennington, Samuel Ward, Gardner Taylor, or S. M. Lockridge. A great deal of emphasis has been placed on preaching and worship in black churches. If a contemporary church planter wishes to alter these traditions, usually careful transition must be made.

CONCERNS FOR CONTEMPORARY PREACHING

As pastors in the black church develop a philosophy of preaching, it is most essential that they be concerned about not compromising when it comes to interpretation. Theology need not be black or white, for when properly understood, the Bible speaks of fairness to all people. The African-American pastor must not succumb to ethnic frustrations and black nationalism, which often foster racial divisiveness.

> THEOLOGY NEED NOT BE BLACK OR WHITE, FOR WHEN PROPERLY UNDERSTOOD, THE BIBLE SPEAKS OF FAIRNESS TO ALL PEOPLE.

A growing subculture within the African-American community is promoting a theology that appears to be as disturbing as the one they are reacting to. For example, in a recent edition of *The Final Call* the front-page article was entitled "Is Min. Farrakhan a Messiah?" The article goes on to tell about Louis Farrakhan's visit to First A.M.E. Church in Los Angeles and how Christian ministers were accepting and supporting him. When famous black pastors like Cecil "Chip" Murray give Farrakhan access to their pulpits and declare a determination to work with him, one has to ask which Jesus they are serving.

Farrakhan had been quoted on *The 700 Club* claiming that he was Jesus. At F.A.M.E. he appeared to hedge a bit while still claiming, "I am not the Jesus.... But I hasten to tell you all I am a Jesus. I am 'a' messiah. I am 'a' deliverer and 'a' restorer under His Messiahship."[3] A person whose theology is this far afield cannot possibly be a partner for Christian ministers to align themselves with. The African-American pastor has an inordinate amount of influence over his congregants. They still look to him for guidance and as a role model. Therefore it is imperative that he act responsibly with his charge.

In addition, there is a growing number of black scholars who are proponents of a black theology. These see Jesus as being the God of the oppressed, mainly blacks. Professor James H. Cone believes that black theology is one of liberation and virtually reduces contemporary Christianity to the religion of the socio-economically oppressed. His hermeneutics is decidedly Afrocentric and allows for little or no deviation. In his book *God of the Oppressed*, James H. Cone asserts,

> Because black liberation is the point of departure of my analysis of the gospel of Jesus, I cannot accept a view of reconciliation based on white values.... To understand the biblical view of reconciliation, we must see it in relation to the struggle of freedom in an oppressed society.[4]

THE PROBLEM WITH CLIMBING MOUNTAINS TOGETHER WITH UNBELIEVERS IS THAT SCRIPTURE ADMONISHES THAT LIGHT AND DARKNESS DO NOT COMPLEMENT EACH OTHER (2 COR. 6:14).

The problems with black theology as proposed by black scholars like Cone, Robert A. Bennett, Charles B. Copher, Cornel West, and others is that it tends to be extremely reductionistic. The whole of Scripture is basically reduced to dealing with the black experience. The contemporary church planter must avoid the lure of placing racial pride above spiritual commitment.

SUMMARY

Preaching in any context can be a powerful medium by which to influence people. Recognizing the potential that the preacher has to shape attitudes and behavior, the contemporary pastor is admonished to exercise prudence in the discharge of his pulpit duties. In addition, the black pastor must avoid trying to build a ministry by political intrigue and controversy. No one can deny that Pastor Murray of F.A.M.E. has built an outstanding ministry in Los Angeles, with thousands of congregants to show for it. Even so, if we find ourselves constantly playing to the media (e.g., passing out condoms after worship services or hosting Louis Farrakhan), we must seriously consider whether we are in Christian ministry or some socio-political sphere. When Farrakhan visited Pastor Murray's church, the pastor's spin on it was this: "We are one family. We have one mountain and many ways to climb it. . . . Can't we climb it together?"[5]

The problem with climbing mountains together with unbelievers is that Scripture admonishes that light and darkness do not complement each other (2 Cor. 6:14). When prominent African-American pastors model such behavior, not only their immediate congregations but other congregations also are influenced.

mission emphases of african-american churches

And you will be my witnesses in Jerusalem, and in all Judea and Samaria, and to the ends of the earth.

—Acts 1:8

the need for missions

There are few ministries that require greater attention in the contemporary black church than a planned and effective approach to missions. The church planter will do well to define and promulgate a strategy for missions at inception. Thereafter missions should be emphasized regularly. A classic mistake that new churches make is to assume that a consciousness for missions will develop as the church grows. Frankly, the longer it takes to get people on board, the less enthusiasm the church may have for missions.

When I became involved in the planting of Emmaus Baptist, we decided to support a number of missions from the very beginning. The adult ministries supported Fishermen Gospel Ministries and Missionaries of the Southwest Baptist Conference. We also supported several individuals who were missionaries. The children's ministry supported World Vision. Children were involved in community projects in the summer and on holidays. The church has supported several African pastors who have been students in the United States. We wanted to impress upon the congregation the need to begin serving others, even though we had little. The biblical principle of being faithful over a few things must be taught early (Matt. 25:21).

Unfortunately, too many churches have no developed plan for global missions or even local evangelism. Such absence of vision must not be allowed to persist in the contemporary church plant. An appreciation for the spiritual and economic conditions of people in our world is sufficient motivation for churches to develop strategies for outreach. Each congregation will have to determine the extent and compass of its mission efforts. Yet if leaders do not take charge and emphasize missions, a church can continue indefinitely without responding to the need. I have been on staff in two churches that had no policy regarding missions and little, if any, such vision.

> UNFORTUNATELY, TOO MANY CHURCHES HAVE NO DEVELOPED PLAN FOR GLOBAL MISSIONS OR EVEN LOCAL EVANGELISM. SUCH ABSENCE OF VISION MUST NOT BE ALLOWED TO PERSIST IN THE CONTEMPORARY CHURCH PLANT.

EARLY MISSIONARY ENDEAVORS

Although some African-American missionary endeavors were carried on in the 1700s, the greatest efforts by African-Americans were realized during the second wave of Protestant missions in the late 1800s. Many people went abroad, mainly to Africa, some independently and others under denominational colors. Still, a relatively small proportion of black Christians served as mission-aries. This was due primarily to a lack of money and their not wanting to suffer additional hardships. In this vein Wilmore writes,

> Although the black denominations wanted to maintain a healthy missionary enterprise outside the country, their aspirations far exceeded their ability to do so. . . . The demands upon the nickel and dime collections in the churches of the blacks were overwhelming. Normal requirements for building national denominations and strengthening home missions to care for the steadily mounting tide moving northward and into the southern cities drained off both personnel and funds.[1]

During this time of expanded mission outreach overseas from all of the denominations in America, a great migration of blacks from the rural areas of the south into the cities of the north occurred. This migration caused a tremendous growth in the number of black churches in the United States, and these churches found themselves financially strapped while try-ing to care for the migrants. Foreign missions floundered.

The church must not wait for major mission developments before taking action. We must build upon established struc-tures. Richard Gray's observation and insight into early mission efforts was that

> African America did not stream to the foreign field. Yet many examples can be cited such as George Liele, a for-mer slave, who ministered throughout Georgia until the death of his former owner. At the death of his former owner during the Revolutionary War, Liele fled to the Caribbean. There he continued missionary work in Jamaica, which resulted in the first black Baptist congre-gation in the Caribbean. Significant missional contributions

during this period were made by the likes of Henry H. Gar-
net, Alexander Crummell, David Walker and Henry M.
Turner. Later, in 1821 Lott Carey sailed to Liberia, West
Africa, where he served as the first African American missionary to Africa. He founded the First Baptist Church,
which is still extant. He was well received.[2]

Mustering up a vibrant mission thrust on a global scale has
always been an extraordinary task.

tHe scope of missions

Missions has to be addressed both on the local and the foreign
fields. Usually, we think of missions as being overseas; however, many people groups exist in our own backyards, where
we can begin to send out missionaries. We must challenge our
own church members to become missionaries, and we must
support them. Those who take the challenge must be
applauded and encouraged often. As the contemporary church
develops a commitment to local missions, the church stands
to benefit. It will be seen as being a caring and genuine influence in its community. The witness of the church in its neighborhood will be elevated. Furthermore, the local mission field
can prove to be a major proving ground from which to launch
world missions.

For too long the black church has seen missions as a circle
of elderly women who fellowship among themselves. At best,
groups of this kind will meet for prayer and Bible study. They
may on occasion visit hospitals and convalescent homes to
deliver some cheer. This is all well and good. I applaud them
for their efforts. Still, leadership must advance a more vigor-
ous vision for missions in the future if the vast number of lost
in the urban context are going to be reached. We have to get
people involved where people are. They will not come to us in

sufficient numbers to make an impact. We have to train and send our people into the streets, parks, gyms, projects, sporting events, and schools.

Wherever there are people, we must have the vision to make inroads. I am on the board of directors of Christian Released Time Education in Los Angeles (CRTE). Children are taken out of class for an hour weekly for religious instruction. The state allows for release time for religious purposes, yet many churches and schools do not take advantage of it. The directors and some of the teachers are serving at Emmaus Baptist. Many children are exposed to the gospel message at an early age through this ministry.

The church must find new and creative ways of reaching people with the gospel message. Mission efforts need to be well planned. Future missions must involve reaching the lost with the Gospel and helping them to cope with life in general. Opportunities for missions abound; we must capitalize on them.

> We have to get people involved where people are.... We have to train and send our people into the streets, parks, gyms, projects, sporting events, and schools. Wherever there are people, we must have the vision to make inroads.

the challenge of missions

Let's face it, missions is challenging in several ways. It takes time and commitment to learn the culture of a people group. Even when one learns to speak their language, he may find that their culture and values are very different. In order to best minister to a people, the missionary must become socially engaged with them. A shift in one's paradigm may be necessary. For example, if we are going to minister to a different racial group or to addicts, homosexuals, or gang members, we must begin to see them simply as lost people. If we cannot overcome our prejudices about them, our mission to them will certainly fail. Therefore leadership must model, train, and equip people with the skills necessary to the task.

summary

There are expansive untapped mission fields, both locally and abroad, that the contemporary church planter is concerned with. Again, in the urban context we have a variety of subcultures—black Muslims, black Israelis, psychics, gangsters, and more. These can be so different that reaching them is tantamount to cross-cultural ministry. We must recognize this fact if any real difference is to be realized. Of course, we must be concerned with foreign missions. I am presently involved in an effort to send a Nigerian friend back to Mali in order to survey it as a potential mission field. Mali is in West Africa and is 98 percent Muslim. He will also be sent to Nigeria in an attempt to develop a cadre of missionaries from Nigeria to minister in Mali. They must learn French and study the culture first.

There are a number of creative ways that the contemporary church planter can get involved in foreign missions if such a vision is a priority. A proper emphasis on missions will give the new church a basis for growth and a focus that is in keeping with the Great Commission.

Chapter Eight

SOCIOLOGICAL PERSPECTIVES OF THE AFRICAN - AMERICAN CHURCH

It is a matter of continuous surprise that churches in America's large urban communities are able to compete with secular interests and to emerge even stronger than the church in rural areas.

—St. Clair Drake

THE CHURCH IN COMMUNITY

The African-American church has played a tremendously important role in serving its people over the last century. In this chapter we will further explore some of the sociological perspectives that account for the differences that we may observe in the black church.

In chapter 3 we looked at some of the theories regarding the existence of the black church. These models are used to explain what the role of the church has been and the reasons for various developments. For example, the compensatory model illustrates how the church has served to give to the masses the acclaim and status that they could not get in the larger society. Although this has been true, such simplified models tend to be too myopic. The church's role has been much more comprehensive.

The contemporary church planter must capitalize on the church's strengths and see its weaknesses as opportunities for ministry. As new churches are planted, we must hold on to the profitable and release that which is simply tradition (1 Thess. 5:21).

The black church has played a comprehensive and multifaceted role in its community. Primarily this has been necessary because many avenues for social, economic, and political expressions were closed to African-Americans. The future of the development of society in politics and economics will determine how important the church's traditional role will continue to be. As blacks and other minorities become assimilated into society at large, the multifaceted role of the church may lessen.

> THE CONTEMPORARY CHURCH PLANTER MUST CAPITALIZE ON THE CHURCH'S STRENGTHS AND SEE ITS WEAKNESSES AS OPPORTUNITIES FOR MINISTRY.

Although there have been significant strides made in academia, politics, entertainment, and employment, there will undoubtedly remain a prominent place for the church to occupy for some time to come. A recent article in the magazine *Black Enterprise* reported on the one hundred largest black businesses in America. Companies from a wide range of industries are doing exceptionally well. For instance, the magazine reported that Karl Kani Infinity, a clothier, ranked twenty-fifth on the list with sales of $59 million.[1] With such success, many are finding less need to turn to the church for aid and comfort. Some of the advances made over the past several decades may present a challenge for the church to look at its role in different ways.

Sociologically speaking, we may conclude that the church's role has involved the religious aspect, being the central institution and the dialectical model holding polar opposites in tension.

tHe ReLiɢious aspect

As we would expect, the church has had the responsibility for the transmission of religious education to its people. The worldview of African-Americans has been shaped by both their African heritage and their conversion to Christianity in America. Rudolf Otto believed that the religious dimension consisted of human beings encountering the sacred, or divine. However, the culture in which this encounter takes place must be considered. Culture in this context relates to the sum of the options for creative survival and expression of a people. As Emile Durkheim puts it, "Above all, religion is ... a social phenomenon, a shared group experience that has shaped and influenced the cultural screens of human communication and interpretation."[2]

The contemporary church planter must appreciate the sociological rationale for the existence of the black church. Otherwise a misinterpretation regarding the development of the church's comprehensive role and position in society may result. More church scholars are beginning to recognize the unique state of the black church and not to interpret it as a mere aberration. As Lincoln reports in this connection,

> It has been only in the past twenty years that scholars of African American history, culture, and religion have begun to recognize that black people created their own unique and distinctive forms of culture and worldviews as parallels rather than replications of the culture in which they were involuntary guests.[3]

The astute church planter will do his research on all pertinent levels before attempting to plant a church in the African-American context.

For the black church, God as ultimately revealed in Christ Jesus dominated the sacred cosmos. Although black Christians and white Christians have the same orthodox beliefs, differences in emphasis and nuance given to certain theological views are evident. The Old Testament's themes of an avenging, conquering, liberating champion are still prevalent among black congregations. The older the congregation or the more elderly, the more likelihood a demand for such exciting imagery in preaching will be.

THE CONTEMPORARY CHURCH PLANTER MUST UNDERSTAND THAT A QUALITATIVELY DIFFERENT CULTURAL FORM OF EXPRESSING CHRISTIANITY IS FOUND IN MOST BLACK CHURCHES, REGARDLESS OF DENOMINATION.

Many black churches still expect to achieve what W. E. B. DuBois referred to as "the frenzy," in which intense enthusiasm and open display of emotions are expressed en masse. A failure to deliver on such experience may result in polite comments like "good talk" or "good lecture." Recall my experience in Monticello, Florida, when the deacon said, "Today he taught, maybe tomorrow he will preach."

The contemporary church planter must understand that a qualitatively different cultural form of expressing Christianity is found in most black churches, regardless of denomination, even now.

THE CENTRAL INSTITUTION

As I indicated before, the African-American church played a central role in many aspects of its people's lives. Undoubtedly, the church has been the most viable and stable institution in the black paraculture. I prefer to use the term *paraculture* to *subculture* to indicate a culture alongside the other cultures in America.

The idea of a subculture indicates that which is under or below and may convey the wrong value judgment. Indeed, churches and mutual-aid societies were the first institutions formed by quasi-free blacks. In 1787, Richard Allen and Absalom Jones founded the Free African Society, a mutual-aid society, which gave birth to Mother Bethel A.M.E. Church in 1794. During Reconstruction the pattern of the church as central institution was solidified when slaves left the plantation as a community base.

Churches, some of which still exist, such as Mother Bethel of Philadelphia, Mother Zion, and Abyssinian Baptist of New York, became the centers of activity for their communities. It is interesting that the church gave rise to other institutions such as banks, insurance companies, schools, and low-income housing and provided an arena for political action. In addition, the church encouraged cultural expressions such as dance, storytelling, humor, music, and drama. The black historian E. Franklin Frazier's apt expression "nation within a nation" demonstrates the multifarious levels of community involvement found in the black church.[4]

The advent of the twentieth century saw the development of black secular organizations such as fraternities and sororities, the NAACP in 1909, the National Urban League in 1911, and independent newspapers—organizations that gave some relief to the church as being the central institution. The twentieth century has seen the birth of a vast number of social, religious, and political groups in which people have found outlets for their needs outside of the church. Nevertheless, the church remains an inextricable component of the culture and experience of the African-American community.

THE DIALECTICAL MODEL

This sociological model represents the idea that black churches are involved in a constant series of dialectical tensions. There is said to be a constant shifting between such polarities. The tension alluded to in this context derives from a desire to participate in two apparently opposite spheres. Such tension was recognized by W. E. B. DuBois in his expression of a "double consciousness" as related to blacks in America. An example of this is a desire for assimilation and a desire to maintain cultural identity. This model helps to explain many of the peculiarities of the black church in a more comprehensive way than some other models do.

If the African-American church planter recognizes this dynamic continuum and understands how it changes in response to social conditions, it will help him to understand the church. One may avoid such misinterpretations as Manning Marable's political assessment of the church as being the "Ambiguous Black Church." Gayraud Wilmore's understanding of this dialectic was most apparent when he described the church as "the most conservative" and "the most radical" institution at the same time.[5]

SUMMARY

The six dialectics referred to in chapter 3 are the key concepts that help to explain the church from a sociological viewpoint. There are other considerations, such as the politics of male versus female, for example. Regardless of the polarity, the most important component of the model is the principle of dialectical tensions and constant interactions as explanations of the sociological aspects of the black church in society.

economic factors in african-american churches

We have all the things that enable us to do what we need to do. We just need to know how to use them.

—African proverb

economic potential

The contemporary church planter must consider how economics figure in the equation. Presently, the black middle class has grown to make up about 25 percent of the African-American population. Yet there are a considerable number of people who are living marginal lives economically. In view of this, what adjustments must one make and what foresight must one possess in order to plant a church with optimal results?

It is incumbent upon pastors and community leaders to impress upon people just how much spending power is available, when considered collectively. A recent cover story in the magazine *Black Enterprise* stated that blacks earn over $400 billion annually. A black married couple, both college graduates, earns an average of $73,443, whereas a similar white couple earns $87,126. Regarding single women with a college degree, blacks average $43,486 compared to $42,685 for whites. Clearly, being a college graduate is a major boost to economic freedom. For this reason, more people must be encouraged and assisted in the pursuit of higher education. Even so, if resources are not used in a strategic manner, little progress will be experienced.[1]

The primary reason for planting a new church is to help the people who are being ministered to. This means assisting them in both their spiritual and their physical needs. But let me caution the church leaders that an inordinate demand for money can lead to despair and distrust by the church community. I have been to several churches in which at least three offerings were taken in a single service! Indeed, in one church I visited, the pastor caused the people to parade around the aisles as they brought their offerings to the altar. Further, they were called up in turns based on the amount of money being given; for example, the $100 people, the $75, $50, $25, and so on. This is both exploitive and without biblical foundation (Matt. 6:1–4).

If such practices are observed, you will undoubtedly get larger offerings on a consistent basis, and thus more money will be available to pay salaries and to build buildings. However, given the instructions of Jesus and the ethical considerations of manipulating people in this way, we must not institute such practices in our new churches, and we must discontinue them where they exist in our older churches.

fUNDING tHE mINIStRy

What shall we do in order to supply our churches with the necessary resources? I believe that we must dare to trust God by being obedient and not simply expedient. I believe that expediency will yield quicker results in terms of funding and growth in other areas of church development. Yet the church's integrity will inevitably be called into question if unacceptable practices are allowed.

We must begin to earnestly teach our people the biblical principles of stewardship. This can be done in seminars, sermons, literature, and most importantly in practice. The church must not be seen as a "rip-off" institution. When multiple offerings are taken and little or no explanation is given for such excesses, the community will naturally think that the pastor is using the church for financial gratification.

> WHAT SHALL WE DO IN ORDER TO SUPPLY OUR CHURCHES WITH THE NECESSARY RESOURCES? I BELIEVE THAT WE MUST DARE TO TRUST GOD BY BEING OBEDIENT AND NOT SIMPLY EXPEDIENT.

New churches must seek help from other churches and denominational organizations, especially in the first couple of years. In a survey of pastors who had planted churches in the black community, only two of the respondents indicated that they had received financial assistance from another organization.

We must determine why churches are reluctant to give assistance to new churches. It is strongly suspected that a key reason is that many new churches start because of tension and splitting from the mother church without her blessing. Such a plant was not planned by an established church or denomination. Again, in the survey of church plants, it was found that only one was started with the blessing of another church, and only one had denominational support, and that for only six months. Out of fifteen churches, thirteen had no outside assistance. This may account for some of the questionable means of raising funds. In addition to high pressure tactics during the offering, too many urban churches resort to fish fries, clothing sales, barbecues, garage sales, and the like to raise funds.

People must be taught that giving is indeed an integral part of worship and that God's people are not to be out begging, in effect, for support. The contemporary church planter will do well to remember Gregory Reed's assessment regarding giving:

> God nowhere in His Word says that His Churches are to have sales, raffles, or bazaars to raise money for their work. God does not want His children to be beggars, going out in the world asking for means to carry on.[2]

I recognize that these are offensive words to some churches in the black community. Perhaps there are also other communities that will benefit from this timely advice. Beyond teaching people to give their tithes and offerings on a consistent basis, urban church leaders must teach their members the benefit of pooling their resources.

> BEYOND TEACHING PEOPLE TO GIVE THEIR TITHES AND OFFERINGS ON A CONSISTENT BASIS, URBAN CHURCH LEADERS MUST TEACH THEIR MEMBERS THE BENEFIT OF POOLING THEIR RESOURCES.

Progressive churches must consider optional ways of creating their financial resources and managing them. For example, members should be encouraged to make endowments through wills and trusts. More churches are participating in credit unions, honor gifts, community development corporations, and joint ventures. Through community-development efforts, churches can work toward neighborhood development, business development, and the establishment of institutes for training in skills. These ventures have the potential for elevating the status of the community and giving many a chance for gainful employment. In turn, as the community grows, people will have more to give to the church's ministry.

We must impress upon the church community that many of its economic problems can be solved by rethinking the way finances are utilized.

modeling economic development

Although church-based community revitalization may sound theoretical, a number of progressive black churches are engaged in that endeavor already. Shiloh Baptist in Washington D.C. is but one such example. In 1982 this church built a Family Life Center at the cost of $5.5 million to deal with the urban problems of the depressed Shaw ghetto. Shiloh has been instrumental in ministering to youths, gang members, drug abusers, and adolescent parents as well as tutoring and being engaged in a variety of similar urban efforts. Other churches like 12th Street Baptist in Detroit, Memorial A.M.E. Zion in Rochester, Ward A.M.E. in Los Angeles, and many progressive churches are socially engaged in their communities.[3]

The contemporary church planter must observe the needs of the community and develop ways and means of addressing them. This will increasingly necessitate cooperative ventures with other churches and organizations.

understanding the economics of the community

The church planter must appreciate the gravity of the effect of a poor economic basis on his community. There is an African proverb that says, "The man who has bread to eat does not appreciate the severity of a famine."

A case in point is the Flint, Michigan, community surrounding the Second Baptist Church after the closing of the Oldsmobile plant there. When the plant closed, most of the residents in the Second Baptist Church community became unemployed. Within a year of the plant's closing, a remarkable increase in requests for aid and assistance was reported by the church's staff. Also, there was a notable increase in the need for pastoral ministry and counseling. When people came to the church's soup kitchen for food, they often sought counseling as well. Wives often reported that their husbands were being physically abusive to them and their children. Many children were being neglected. For example, youths were reporting to the youth pastor that their parents were spending money on pleasures like alcohol and drugs, instead of on food for them.

> CHURCH LEADERS MUST UNDERSTAND THE DEVASTATION THAT ECONOMIC PAUCITY BRINGS TO THE FAMILIES IN THE CHURCH COMMUNITY.

Another problem related to the plant closure was that many older persons were forced to retire earlier than expected. They were not prepared for the abrupt change, and consequently, a higher incidence of depression was reported among seniors in the church community. Other forms of social deterioration and violence like rape and assault also increased during this time. Second Baptist responded wisely to the situation by establishing support systems, including a lay counseling ministry. The pastoral staff was overwhelmed with problem situations after the plant closure.

IMPLICATIONS OF CHALLENGED ECONOMICS

As economic and social problems continue to afflict the African-American community, affected families will reach out to the black church for help. Church leaders must understand the devastation that economic paucity brings to the families in the church community. Colleen Birchett indicated that there are four basic issues that critically affect the African-American family:

1. The roles we want our children to play in our community in particular and in the society in general when they become adults.

2. The training of our children, which was traditionally done by the family and is now progressively declining.

3. The miseducation or lack of education of African-American children in the nation's school systems. (Read Carter Woodson's book *The Miseducation of the Negro*.)

4. The general breakdown of the African-American nuclear and extended family.[4]

Birchett sees these as being basic but critical matters for the church to face if its people are going to be effectively helped.

summary

So then, as the economic noose tightens, as in the case of the Oldsmobile layoff, problems are exacerbated and require an increasingly higher level of support and skill. The contemporary church leader must be able to assist couples in adjusting to ego differences. Men and women must see their differences as complementary and not necessarily as conflicting. Couples must be helped to adjust to changes in male and female roles.

Many households have working mothers and nonworking fathers. In addition, women are taking on nontraditional roles in general. The church can help families to make meaningful adjustments here. Also, couples need to be encouraged to be flexible. Often women are better educated and have better skills. This may lead to more women being employed. In this context men and the extended family will have to take on roles that allow the family to function. Often black families do not look like others or function as they do. Nevertheless, many function well, while others are struggling against significant challenges.

Chapter Ten

the hostility factor in the african-american community

> To know one's self is wisdom, but to know one's neighbor is genius.
> —Minna Antrim

why the tension persists

A number of developments have led to the perennial tension that the urban communities have with society at large. Arguably, some of the theories offered to explain this state of affairs have some validity while others are less credible. At any rate, the urban church planter must not deny the potential role that racial tension and ethnicity play in his community. It would be good to be able to say that ethnicity is a nonissue today. However, both black and white extremists continue to operate at a fever pitch in an effort to thwart any meaningful social progress.

ADDRESSING THE ISSUES

It is quite troubling to consider that in the eighteen months prior to June 1996 over thirty southern black churches were burned down. It is also troubling to see racial tension being heightened by the rhetoric of Black Muslims and other militant groups. It is of equal concern that the church as a whole does not decry this evil with one voice. Admittedly, forgiveness is a prerequisite to real reconciliation, and the most natural arena for this to occur has to be the Christian church. If we as a nation are to rectify or alleviate our race problems, the church must assume its lead as a role model.

> FORGIVENESS IS A PREREQUISITE TO REAL RECONCILIATION, AND THE MOST NATURAL ARENA FOR THIS TO OCCUR HAS TO BE THE CHRISTIAN CHURCH.

There are many anxious and disheartened people among all communities. An approach characterized by attack and counterattack has gone on long enough, and still the blame game prevails, in which one ethnic group blames another for its situation. The contemporary leader needs to understand that the church is in a pivotal position to make substantial contributions if careful planning and consideration are to be given to the plight of its community. James A. Joseph's insight into the influence of the church was that

> the black church is in a position to have a much wider impact. Its future role in the black community will depend to a large degree on whether or not it proves capable of reading the pulse of the times.[1]

Joseph correctly observes that the church must be able to capitalize on the times. He recognizes the frustrations of youths and their growing lack of interest in the church. He continues,

Most black youth are alienated from the church not because they are immoral but because they are too moral for the static moralism now being proclaimed. The black church can no longer simply preach what is moral without joining men in doing what is moral.[2]

Of course, this is true for the church at large. There are many who feel that they are on the fringes and left out of the mainstream. This situation has the potential for anarchy if it is not dealt with appropriately in the near future. If our people's level of consciousness about solutions to the social and economic problems is going to be elevated, the church must take charge. The church needs to be actively involved in all aspects of society. Only then will a more enlightened populace evolve from the shadows of ignorance and hate.

> THE CHURCH NEEDS TO BE ACTIVELY INVOLVED IN ALL ASPECTS OF SOCIETY. ONLY THEN WILL A MORE ENLIGHTENED POPULACE EVOLVE FROM THE SHADOWS OF IGNORANCE AND HATE.

Several decades ago many youths would at least go to church to appease their parents. Now fewer young people will even pretend that they are committed to the church, and many do not attend. So then, the church planter is beset with the arduous task of reaching unchurched youths; yet he must do so if significant inroads are going to be made into the community.

Developing interest centers has been applauded as a way of reaching urban youths. Interest centers are being developed in an attempt to make relevant the ministry of the church. In other words, it is an effort to reach people where they are. The church has been seen as irrelevant by many blacks, especially men, for several decades. According to Walter A. McCray, interest centers serve to

actively involve young adults in programs that would better equip them to enter the job market. Another [pur-
pose] could be to serve as a center of informal education
and information sharing. Interest centers could also serve
the purpose of inspiring and challenging the young adults
to exercise their creativity and productiveness.[3]

Given the magnitude of social problems that many urban communities experience, interest groups may offer an alternative to
idleness and delinquency.

Interest centers can be developed as off-campus facilities
where counseling, job training, tutoring, job referrals, and self-
help projects can be advanced. Light production could be
engaged in for a profit to be shared by those in the interest center, such as the manufacturing of crafts, hair-braiding, T-shirt
designing, sewing, and recycling. Such centers may act as the
necessary catalyst to propel some of the idle and disenchanted
youths into a new level of confidence and esteem.

The more the church planter knows about his community,
the better will be his service to it. A number of sociological theories have been suggested to account for the generally lower
social status of African-Americans. Some theories are said to
be conservative and others are liberal.

CONSERVATIVE SOCIAL THEORIES

Conservative theories are based on either discrimination
in the marketplace or judgments made in the minds of people.
Cornel West has suggested three basic versions of the conservative camps: the market version, the sociobiologist version,
and the culturalist version.

Briefly, the market version indicates that those who have the
means (capitalists) see blacks from an irrational viewpoint.
They have "bad tastes" about blacks. This leads to discrimina-

tion in employment opportunities. The apparent solution to the problem occasioned by this view is for the capitalist to see that profits would be maximized by discarding discrimination in the workplace. Milton Friedman's classic *Capitalism and Freedom* (1962) and Gary Becker's renowned *Economics of Discrimination* (1957) support this contention.

The sociobiologist version holds that blacks are in some sense inferior to whites. Proponents of this version use IQ performance, which allegedly measures intelligence, as evidence for their view. Arthur Jensen, *Harvard Educational Review* (Winter 1969), and Richard Hernstein, *Atlantic Monthly* (September 1971), are proponents of such a theory.

The culturalist version also maintains the view that whites are superior to blacks. However, they say their theory is based on cultural rather than biological characteristics. Adherents to this view claim that habits for success such as patience, persistence, hard work, and willingness to defer gratification are underdeveloped in African-American culture. Obviously, the solution here is for blacks to adopt these habits. Ostensibly, then all of the community's problems would be eradicated.

Liberal social theories

Generally, liberals reject mere persuasion to change "tastes" or attitudes. Their focus is on two domains: the barriers in the marketplace and inhibitions in the African-American culture. These people may be seen as "market liberals" and "culturalist liberals."

Market liberals assert that government intervention is necessary to insure that fair criteria are applied in the employment and firing of black workers. This will allow for economic parity. Sociologist Gunnar Myrdal and economist Paul Samuelson supported this theory.

Furthermore, culturists like Thomas Pettigrew hold that government programs should be established to train people, especially African-Americans, for jobs. Both the conservative and the liberal social engineers see either the marketplace or the cultural (educational) aspects of the black culture as being the solution to the community's ills. As Cornel West says regarding conservatives and liberals,

> Both groups assume that "rough justice" between blacks and white Americans can be achieved if black productivity is given its rightful due, namely, if there is close parity in black and white incomes.[4]

MORE THAN ECONOMICS

Although there is a need for economic parity in a number of areas, the cultural differences cannot be explained simply as a matter of economics. In addition, there are historical factors, myths, social stigmata, and other cultural considerations that are not accounted for in these theories.

Many people in our society have a sense of hopelessness and see the hegemony of the system as being overwhelming. Their ineffectual status, real or imagined, may contribute to rage and anger. Unless the church understands and deals with this anxiety in the community, social and economic issues may never be resolved. In his work *Race Matters*, West declared,

> Malcolm X's pessimism about the capacity and possibility of white Americans to shed their racism led him, ironically, to downplay the past and present bonds between blacks and whites. For if the two groups were, as Martin Luther King, Jr., put it, locked into "one garment of destiny," then the very chances for black freedom were nil.[5]

Should this kind of reasoning continue to be cultivated, the chasm between the races will expand. Contemporary church planters are charged to seek viable alternatives for bringing people together. Respect for self and one another is essential. This mutual respect will require manpower and spiritual power of a high magnitude.

> RESPECT FOR SELF AND ONE ANOTHER IS ESSENTIAL. THIS MUTUAL RESPECT WILL REQUIRE MANPOWER AND SPIRITUAL POWER OF A HIGH MAGNITUDE.

SUMMARY

It is important to acknowledge social and cultural differences among ethnic groups. However, a serious attempt to understand the causation of cultural norms needs to be undertaken on a continuous basis. A more enlightened view of oneself and others will undoubtedly lead to better human relations. Still, the theories employed to explain society must be based on an objective system of fairness, honesty, and truth. Many biblical examples can be effectively used to draft guidelines in this regard.

the homogeneous principle in african-american churches

The strength of the wolf is in the pack.

—Rudyard Kipling

understanding the homogeneous principle

Since the United States has been built primarily with immigrants from many different countries, we have a unique composite of cultures living in tandem. This cultural variety can enrich society, but it also accounts for social barriers. Unless these barriers are recognized and understood, exchange between different ethnic groups will be largely ineffective.

Church growth proponents have identified a correlation between different kinds of churches and four types or levels of evangelism. E–0 evangelism is concerned with those who are of the same culture as the church or mission agency involved in outreach. No major barrier is erected between the evangelist and the pre-Christian (except perhaps a spiritual one). This is usually the easiest target group to reach because there is commonality between the persons involved.

In E–1 evangelism only one barrier has to be crossed to reach an unbeliever. For example, it will be necessary to cross a religious, language, social, or cultural barrier to effectively communicate the gospel to an E–1 person. Generally there is not a high degree of difference at this level.

However, with E–2 evangelism two barriers must be negotiated. This makes it more difficult to reach someone with the gospel because there is less commonality between the persons involved. Again, the barriers may be religious or cultural.

Now, in E–3 evangelism the evangelist is faced with three or more barriers. This is a very complex level of evangelism. In E–2 and especially E–3 evangelism, a mother church (or mission agency) will often plant new congregations among people who are from totally different racial, linguistic, social, geographic, or cultural backgrounds from the church planter. By identifying these types of evangelism, the planter can plan an effective strategy to reach the targeted group.[1]

> CULTURAL VARIETY CAN ENRICH SOCIETY, BUT IT ALSO ACCOUNTS FOR SOCIAL BARRIERS.

How can the church planter, who is concerned with church growth, overcome social barriers? Should this be a concern at all? Some church-growth proponents believe that the homogeneous unit principle is key to reaching people who have similar backgrounds. According to the homogeneous principle, people like to become Christians "without having to cross racial, linguistic, or class barriers to do so."[2] Basically, this means that the contemporary church planter must determine who his target audience is and concentrate on reaching it.

As a practical matter, the homogeneous principle is a reality in America. Someone has suggested that the most segregated hour in the week is 11:00 on Sunday morning. No one can argue convincingly that people are not generally more comfortable with "their own kind" of people. Most of the black churches that I have visited are predominantly black, and many are 100 percent so.

It is interesting that blacks and whites congregated together more often in the late 1700s and early 1800s than during post–Civil War times. Indeed, many African-Americans were not permitted to worship outside the presence of a white congregation unless an overseer was at least in attendance. Nevertheless, blacks did in effect "steal away" into the forests or other areas for clandestine worship. The African Methodist Episcopal church began in 1816 when black ministers Richard Allen and Absalom Jones broke away from the Methodists because they did not feel comfortable in the white congregation.

> IN EARLIER TIMES WHITES AND BLACKS FOUND OCCASION TO MEET TOGETHER MORE OFTEN THAN IS COMMONLY ACKNOWLEDGED.

After the Civil War, black Baptists left the Southern Baptist Convention mainly because they felt more comfortable with their "own kind" of people. Even so, in earlier times whites and blacks found occasion to meet together more often than is commonly acknowledged. C. Eric Lincoln reports,

> Two black ministers, Josiah Bishop at Portsmouth and William Lemon at Gloucester, are known to have pastored white Baptist churches in Virginia. Nor was it uncommon for black churches to have white pastors. Robert Ryland was the white pastor of the First African Church of Richmond for twenty-five years.[3]

As further attestation to how blacks and whites were obliged to work together, Lincoln continues,

> John Wesley recorded in his Journal that he baptized his first two black converts, one of whom was a woman, on November 29, 1759. Historical records indicate that African Americans were among the charter members of the very first Methodist society which was organized in Frederick County, Maryland, in 1764.[4]

Both Daniel Coker and Francis Asbury were contemporaries of Richard Allen and were fellow laborers with him.

Clearly, misunderstandings and a desire of blacks for autonomy from white hegemony led to a further distancing of black and white in the church. This separation was more comfortable for all. Still, a major concern is whether it is theologically tenable to promote a principle of homogeneity for the sake of expediency and comfort. Would not the unbelieving world be impressed if black and white Christians were more comfortable and cohesive in all our churches? Jesus proclaimed that the world would know that we are His disciples by the love that we have for one another (John 13:35).

In 1976 Montgomery W. Smith did some research on homogeneity as it relates to church growth. As may be expected, he observed the homogeneous principle at work in churches throughout the United States. This led him to postulate,

> Churches tend to be composed of persons of the same social homogeneity. This fact had been identified for some time. As early as 1952 C. H. Dodd had produced a small book entitled, *More Than Doctrine Divides Us*. In this a leading cause of division in the one church of God was social forms clung to in spite of church consequences. The eastern theologian, Niebuhr, had identified the social class base of western denominationalism as early as 1945.[5]

Obviously homogeneity has been a way of life in the United States for some time and will likely continue to be so.

some implications of the homogeneous principle

The church planter must decide whether he is going to be a church-growth pastor. Does he understand and will he use the people approach? That is, will he target a specific geographical area with a strategy designed to reach the people, based on culture and demographics? Perhaps this is too scientific for many.

Indeed, one of the main objections to the church-growth movement has been that it uses sociology as a corollary discipline, whereas theologians have traditionally seen philosophy as cognate to theology. The inference is that church-growth proponents depend on empirical observations (experiences), while theologians tend to depend on the Word as a construct. The former emphasize the "is" versus the "ought." Obviously, this is a simplistic conclusion. As C. Peter Wagner observed in this connection,

> When pushed, many of them [that is, theologians who question church growth theory] would feel comfortable in admitting that the principle has sociological validity, but that it cannot be defended theologically. Few of them would recognize how much they themselves have been influenced by the contemporary social mood of racial equality and the melting pot theory.[6]

Although these theologians would deny that empirical observations are valid constructs upon which to build a theology of church growth, as a practical matter many are influenced by the products of this method. Resolving the tension between the theological and the practical aspects of church growth is an ongoing process.

A balance is called for here. One must remain true to the-ology and still be able to develop a philosophy of ministry that is practical. One failing of the church is an overstatement of facts when it comes to theology, and an understatement when it comes to practical application.

The homogeneous principle has promise as a tool for evangelism. Unbelievers are not obliged to follow biblical principles of love and understanding. They may be reached easier by people who have similar ethnic, linguistic, social, economic, educational background and the like. That is, "their own kind of people." It is also easier for the believer when E–1 evangelism is conducted.

Clearly, church growth is a biblical principle. The church is charged with the task of reaching the lost with the gospel mes-sage of salvation. The methodology of doing so can and should be open to scrutiny. Although I can appreciate the benefits of the homogeneous unit principle, there are some concerns that we must explore.

First, if new believers begin with their "own kind," will they not be inclined to remain with them and thereby perpetuate a segregated Christianity?

Second, will not many see the homogeneous principle as an excuse for not reaching people, simply because of differ-ence in race, religion, language, or the like? Many believers have regular contact with people who may have one or more distinctives. Yet they communicate about many matters such as politics, sports, or family concerns. Why not do the same in matters of religion?

Third, homogeneity may give credence to those who hold a notion of superiority with respect to race, education, lan-guage, or other cultural identifiers. It may offer support to the segregationist efforts in a number of these categories, espe-cially at the popular level of racial superiority.

Finally, as neighborhoods and communities change, churches that do not assimilate their community in an all-inclusive manner will suffer extinction.

The African-American church will benefit from having other ethnic groups better understand it. When people get to know one another in more intimate ways, they will respect and accept one another for who they really are. The exchange of ideas and the giving of mutual aid can be enjoyed. Emmaus Baptist chose to associate with a predominantly white conference for a number of reasons. The main reason was that the Baptist General Conference gave church planting a high priority. This was demonstrated by a relatively high number of churches being planted in the Vietnamese, Latino, African, Anglo, and Filipino communities. We saw this as being progressive. John T. Sisemore felt that church growth should not be confined by barriers. He said,

> CLEARLY, CHURCH GROWTH IS A BIBLICAL PRINCIPLE. THE CHURCH IS CHARGED WITH THE task of REACHING the Lost WITH THE GOSPEL message of salvation. THE METHODOLOGY of DOING SO CAN AND SHOULD BE OPEN to SCRUTINY.

Genuine church growth cannot be contained. It is a phenomenon that leaps over all barriers and crosses all lines of demarcation. For example, when Philip reached out to the Ethiopian eunuch, he moved across both racial lines and religious classifications.[7]

Although most of the churches in the conference remain homogeneous, a number of occasions for working together are provided through mutual association. Of course, some find areas of disagreement; however, face-to-face dialogue is beginning to be experienced. The barriers are being disassembled.

As a result, people are getting to know one another in beneficial ways that would not otherwise be possible.

summary

Homogeneity is one of the most controversial and misunderstood principles of church growth. Although it does have practical applications, it may appear to promote separatism. This is especially true for the uninitiated. Clearly, there is a sense in which the church can benefit from promoting openness and acceptance of all people. This will likely result in a stronger witness for the church in the future. The church will always struggle with sheer pragmatism versus the biblical ideal.

Chapter Twelve

the future of church planting in african-american churches

> We shall not cease from exploration, and the end of all our exploring will be to arrive where we started and know the place for the first time.
>
> —T. S. Eliot

new directions for church planters

I can still remember the first time that as an associate pastor I was assigned to administer communion. The senior pastor was away. He had been the founding pastor and had served for over thirty years. When I made some apparently small deviation from his usual way of conducting the service, an elderly woman of the congregation made sure that I was aware that "Pastor doesn't do it that way." People will often resist change without any more rational reason than that they "never did it that way before." The contemporary church planter must recognize this systemic resistance and still be ready to lead the church into the twenty-first century.

The modern pastor must be equipped to evaluate his particular setting and determine where he needs to go and how best to make the necessary transitions. This may require some experimenting with different worship formats, methods of assimilation, and methods of evangelism and with designing ministries that are relevant to the needs of the people being served. Many of our churches are virtual carbon copies of one another. The successful churches tend to offer something special and novel.

some key PROCEDURES for PROMOTING CHANGE are (1) PLANNING for INTENTIONAL CHURCH GROWTH, (2) DEVELOPING a team APPROACH to MINISTRY, (3) FORMULATING strategies to eLevate family Life, AND (4) ENCOURAGING PRECISE RECORD keePING.

In the future, change will be necessary for the prosperity of the church and the community. The pastor who has older members must be shrewd enough to cultivate a climate that will allow for both the new Christians and the older ones to coexist. Both must be made to feel significant. This may require multiple opportunities for worship services and other ministries.

Some of the key procedures for promoting change in black churches are (1) planning for intentional church growth by planting churches, (2) developing a team approach to ministry, (3) formulating strategies to elevate family life, and (4) encouraging precise record keeping. Although the church is primarily spiritual, its business aspects must not be overlooked. At Emmaus Baptist I have to continually ask the ushers to keep attendance records and the finance committee to provide quarterly statements. People do not seem to appreciate the importance of keeping records in many of our churches. Obviously, this will cause problems for audits, planning, and accountability.

Progressive leadership must teach the importance of change and its relationship to church growth. Recognizing the potential danger associated with change, Leith Anderson wrote,

> When we talk about major changes and human responses, do we risk sinful manipulation of Christ's church? Is it possible that we will adapt to the ways of the world and forsake the ways of the Lord? Is there enormous danger in reshaping the church for the twenty-first century?[1]

Clearly, there are some dangers, as Anderson admits. We run the potential danger of losing our focus on the Lord as we attempt to develop ministries that are people oriented. Therefore contemporary church planters must not make changes outside of the direction of the Holy Spirit as the Word of God is applied (see 2 Tim. 4:3–5).

Intentional Church Planting

Again, in the survey sent to churches that were recently planted in the black community, only two of fifteen responses indicated any support from another source. One of the acknowledged sources of support was a white denomination, and only one was a mother church. I see this trend as being outdated and in need of serious change. Territorialism and overbearing leadership must give way to cooperation and planned support. New church plants must begin with a goal to plant daughter churches within a prescribed time frame. At Emmaus Baptist we plan to be in position to plant another church within three years. In addition, the new churches must have the same vision of planting other churches, by design.

I am acquainted with several churches in Los Angeles and elsewhere that have not grown for years. They have not devised a plan for growth. This indicates a growing need for church consultants in the black community.

Furthermore, the selection of church planters should be based on a pastor's spiritual maturity, his vision for church planting, and his love for people and community. Selection should not be based simply on race or education. Ratliff cautions regarding the importance of making a careful selection of a pastor for a church plant: "The two must be matched economically and socially as much as possible. The homogeneity/heterogeneity principle can be argued convincingly on both sides of the issue...."[2] Being certain of selecting the best possible candidate for planting a given church is most essential to its success.

There are a number of models that the contemporary black church can explore in an effort to seek alternative means of church-planting. I have related that church splitting has been a primary way of starting churches. This method needs no further discussion. It is important to remember that no one model will necessarily fit every church-planting situation. Optional models are necessary. Charles Walz, in his study of church-planting methodology at Fuller Theological Seminary, proposes a number of optional models, discussed below, that may be employed by modern church planters.[3]

1. The first optional model is the spontaneous Christian community method, whereby a group of Christians relating and meeting for some purpose then decide to become chartered as a church. The group's initial reason for existence may have been to form a prayer group or a Bible study, for example.

2. A second means of church planting is by the instigation of church planters, who are purposely selected to plant

churches. These catalytic church planters have no intention of pastoring the new church. Once a group is organized as a church, they call a pastor.

3. A third method of church planting is the mission team. In this instance, a sodality (such as a district extension or a home mission board) plants the new church. Here the team effort is a very prominent aspect of the operation. Parachurch groups are working to plant churches by sending out teams to accomplish the plant.

4. A fourth model to consider is colonization. In colonization, a group of people will move into a community in order to start a church there. It may require a change of employment or residence. An example of colonization is seen in Pastor Frank Radcliffe's move from Amarillo, Texas, to Chicago. He took eleven people with him from Bethany Baptist Church of Amarillo. In six months, the suburban lower-middle-class white community had grown to over one hundred members (a previously neglected group mainly in the affluent area).

5. Adoption is a fifth method of church planting in which a district or denomination becomes related to another congregation. The parent body brings an intern aboard and trains this intern in their philosophy of ministry and prepares him or her for pastoring a new church. This pastor will then be assigned to a church in need of a pastor, or a new church may be planted. The parent body will help to support the adopted church. Grace Community Church of Panorama City, California, has such a program. I am aware of one African-American church being sponsored in this fashion in Inglewood, California.

6. Establishing a daughter church is a sixth model of church planting; it is similar to adoption. In this case, members of a mother church act as a nucleus for the planting of a new church in an intentional manner. The mother church plans and supports the new church. This is one of the easiest and most eco-

nomical ways of planting a church. Actually, colonization and adoption are specified forms of mothering a church. However, "hiving off" is generally a distinguishing mark of daughter churches. This happens when a church finds that it has certain pockets of members already living in an area and plans to make them the core for a new church. It is most important for the church to plan in advance what size and kind of church it is going to be. This will help in the selection of a pastor and in the structuring of the church.

> MEMBERS OF A MOTHER CHURCH ACT AS A NUCLEUS FOR THE PLANTING OF A NEW CHURCH.... THE MOTHER CHURCH PLANS AND SUPPORTS THE NEW CHURCH. THIS IS ONE OF THE EASIEST AND MOST ECONOMICAL WAYS OF PLANTING A CHURCH.

7. The satellite model represents yet a seventh method for the contemporary church planter to consider. In this model there can be either a scattered or a gathered form. In the scattered satellite model several campuses are stationed throughout a city or region, whereas in the gathered satellite a number of churches meet at the same facility but at different times. Nevertheless, in either case the same senior pastor is over all of the congregations concerned. Each may have different undershepherds to assist in the ministry. Yet the various churches do not become autonomous but continue to operate as one church.

8. An eighth model, with multiple campuses, is another option open to contemporary church planters. In this model the same staff serves two or more campuses, usually on a rotational basis. Tim LaHaye established this form of church in San Diego and El Cajon, California. In Birmingham, Alabama, Pastor Frank Barker conducts three services himself at Briarwood Presbyterian Church. Services are held at early, mid-, and late

morning. This method of church planting may be used when current facilities are outgrown and/or the need to reach a new area is evident.

9. Finally, the multicongregational church is a model in which several congregations share the same facilities and administration. Different ethnic congregations may constitute one church. Temple Baptist of Los Angeles has three separate and semi-autonomous congregations. A Spanish and a Korean congregation each has its own pastor, maintains its own culture, and worships separately except once a quarter, when they all meet together with the Anglo congregation. This model may be most applicable in a highly pluralistic community.

> If a CHURCH IS to GROW, the PASTOR MUST EQUIP ABLe peopLe AND ReLease them to DO their woRk, aLBeit with appRopRiate oveRsiGht.

team appRoach to LeadeRship

Unfortunately, many African-American pastors still have a "king's mentality" when it comes to leading the church. Their leadership is practically unquestioned and autonomous. New church pastors must empower the people by helping them to discover their spiritual gifts and use them in service to the community. Clearly, the pastor's authority in the church needs to be established; nevertheless, he must not be seen as the only person capable of leadership in the church.

Plurality of leadership allows for a more complete ministry, qualitatively and quantitatively. If a church is to grow, the pastor must equip able people and release them to do their work, albeit with appropriate oversight.

In one church I was an assistant pastor and assigned to direct the couples ministry. I became frustrated because the senior pastor would not allow anything to occur unless he was present. He was usually in charge of the lesson or session. He was not open to having outside speakers. It became apparent early on that he was, in fact, in charge of the couples ministry. As you may have guessed, I quit after a relatively short period of frustration. In a well-organized church the pastor has oversight of the ministry, but he is not obliged to control every detail of it (2 Tim. 2:2). Such micromanagement leads to the frustration of talented people and stifling of the ministry.

strategies for family ministries

It is fair to say that today many urban families throughout our nation are generally in desperate straits. The prevalence of drugs, unemployment, incarceration, and violent crime demands special approaches to urban ministry. The innovative pastor will devise new and effective ways of attending to these problems in his community. Ministry opportunities abound for the meaningful deployment of the congregation into the world. The trend appears to be continued growth of the black population in urban areas. This trend provides an increasing need for urban ministries. George and Yvonne Abatso believe that

> if the present birth rates continue among African Americans, . . . by the year 2000, Blacks . . . will comprise 1/4 of the U.S. population. Moreover, by the year 2010, it has been predicted that ethnic and racial minorities will comprise the majority population in more than 50 cities.[4]

It is obvious that with this rapid growth more churches with solution-oriented ministries will be required. Otherwise the status of our urban areas will continue to depreciate at an alarming rate. Urban churches will need to work together in order to create work banks, food banks, credit unions, tutoring, Christian education, and other community-based support systems to elevate the family.

keeping statistics

I explained previously that traditionally blacks have enjoyed an oral tradition. However, given the possible legal ramifications of operating a church, audits and accounting are necessary for fiscal responsibility. Generally speaking, better planning will be accomplished if accurate records are maintained regarding attendance, ceremonies, income, and expenditures. The progressive church will appreciate the benefits of keeping accurate records.

summary

The demands on the urban church as a result of population density, social problems, and the scarcity of resources will call for new approaches to ministry. As churches are planted, careful planning and research must be applied to the community involved. Then the church model that is followed and developed may be geared more closely to the needs of the community. The contemporary church planter may design a number of approaches that would best serve the family and the wider community. The modern church must realize a vision that goes beyond the ordinary and must address the real problems of real people.

BIBLIOGRAPHY

Abatso, George, and Yvonne Abatso. *The African American Family*. Chicago: Urban Ministries, 1991.

Anderson, Leith. *A Church for the 21st Century*. Minneapolis: Bethany House, 1992.

Barna, George. *The Power of Vision*. Ventura, Calif.: Regal, 1992.

_____ *User-friendly Churches*. Ventura, Calif.: Regal, 1991.

Barbour, Floyd B., editor. *The Black Seventies*. Boston: Porter Sargent, 1970.

Callahan, Kennon L. *Twelve Keys to an Effective Church*. New York: Harper & Row, 1983.

Cone, James H. *God of the Oppressed*. New York: Harper & Row, 1975.

DeSilva, Ranjit. "An Analysis of Charismatic Leadership in the African American Church in Los Angeles." Ph.D. diss., Fuller Institute, 1994.

Evans, Tony. *Let's Get to Know Each Other*. Nashville: Thomas Nelson, 1995.

Franklin, John H., and Alfred A. Moss Jr. *From Slavery to Freedom*. New York: McGraw-Hill, 1994.

Frazier, Thomas R. *Afro-American History*. Belmont, Calif.: Wadsworth, 1988.

George, Carl F. *Prepare Your Church for the Future*. Old Tappan, N.J.: Revell, 1992.

George, Carl F., and Robert E. Logan. *Leading and Managing Your Church*. Old Tappan, N.J.: Revell, 1987.

Gray, Richard. "The Black Manifest Destiny Motivation for Mission During the Golden Age of Black Nationalism." Ph.D. diss., Fuller Institute, 1996.

Howard, Victor B. *Conscience and Slavery*. Kent, Ohio: Kent State University Press, 1990.

"Is Min. Farrakhan a Messiah?" *The Final Call* (14 May 1996).

Janssen, Al, and Larry K. Weeden. *Seven Promises of a Promise Keeper*. Colorado Springs: Focus on the Family, 1994.

King, Martin Luther, Jr. "I Have a Dream." *Ebony Magazine* (January 1986): 40–42.

Lincoln, C. Eric, and Lawrence H. Mamiya. *The Black Church in the African American Experience*. Durham, N.C.: Duke University Press, 1990.

Lindsell, Harold. *Harper Study Bible*. Grand Rapids: Zondervan, 1985.

Logan, Robert E. *Beyond Church Growth*. Tarrytown, N.Y.: Revell, 1989.

McCray, Walter A. *Black Young Adults*. Chicago: Black Light Fellowship, 1992.

McGavran, Donald, and Win Arn. *How to Grow Your Church*. Ventura, Calif.: Regal, 1973.

Muhammad, Rosalind. "Christian Pastors Defend Min. Farrakhan." *The Final Call* (14 May 1996).

Muhammod, Tariq K. "From Here to Infinity." *Black Enterprise* (June 1996).

Nelson, Hart M., and Anne K. Nelson, *Black Church in the Sixties*. Lexington: University Press of Kentucky, 1975.

Ratliff, Joe S., and Michael J. Cox. *Church Planting in the African-American Community*. Nashville: Broadman, 1993.

Reed, Gregory J. *Economic Empowerment Through the Church*. Grand Rapids: Zondervan, 1994.

Ridley, Charles R. *How to Select Church Planters*. Pasadena, Calif.: Fuller Evangelistic Association, 1988.

Schaller, Lyle E. *Growing Plans*. Nashville: Abingdon, 1983.

_____ *It's a Different World*. Nashville: Abingdon, 1987.

Sisemore, John T. *Church Growth Through the Sunday School*. Nashville: Broadman, 1983.

Smith, Montgomery W. "Homogeneity and American Church Growth." Ph.D. diss., Fuller Institute, 1976.

Wagner, C. Peter. *Church Growth State of the Art*. Wheaton: Tyndale House, 1986.

_____ *Leading Your Church to Growth*. Ventura, Calif.: Regal, 1984.

Walz, Charles W. "Church Planting and the Mission of the Church." Ph.D. diss., Fuller Institute, 1984.

West, Cornel. *Keeping the Faith*. New York: Routledge, 1993.

_____ *Race Matters*. New York: Vintage Books, 1993.

Whigham-De'sir, Marjorie. "The Real Black Power." *Black Enterprise* (July 1996).

Wilmore, Gayraud S., editor. *African American Religious Studies*. Durham, N.C.: Duke University Press, 1989.

_____ *Black America and the Black Radicalism: An Interpretation of the Religious History of Afro-American People*. Maryknoll, N.Y.: Orbis, 1992.

Woodson, Carter G. *The History of the Negro Church*. Washington, D.C.: Associated Publishers, 1945.

notes

Chapter One: A Different World

1. Al Janssen and Larry K. Weeden, *Seven Promises of a Promise Keeper* (Colorado Springs: Focus on the Family, 1994), 9.

2. Martin Luther King Jr., "I Have A Dream," *Ebony* (January 1986): 40–42.

Chapter Two: How African-American Churches Are Planted

1. Names, places, and details have been changed to protect privacy.

2. Robert E. Logan, *Beyond Church Growth* (Tarrytown, N.Y.: Revell, 1989), 74.

3. Charles R. Ridley, *How to Select Church Planters* (Pasadena, Calif.: Fuller Evangelistic Association, 1988), 5–6.

Chapter Three: Why African-American Churches Are Different From Anglo Churches

1. Tony Evans, *Let's Get to Know Each Other* (Nashville: Thomas Nelson, 1995), 2.

2. C. Eric Lincoln and Lawrence H. Mamiya, *The Black Church in the African American Experience* (Durham, N.C.: Duke University Press, 1990), 17.

3. Hart M. and Anne K. Nelsen, *Black Church in the Sixties* (Lexington: University Press of Kentucky, 1975).

4. Lincoln and Mamiya, *The Black Church in the African American Experience,* 16.

5. Ibid., 15.

Chapter Four: Leadership in African-American Churches

1. Carter G. Woodson, *The History of the Negro Church* (Washington, D.C.: Associated Publishers, 1945), 242.

2. Ranjit DeSilva, "An Analysis of Charismatic Leadership in the African American Church in Los Angeles" (Ph.D. diss., Fuller Institute, 1994), 109.

3. Joe S. Ratliff and Michael J. Cox, *Church Planting in the African-American Community* (Nashville: Broadman, 1993), 9.

4. Ibid., 10.

5. Leith Anderson, *A Church for the 21st Century* (Minneapolis: Bethany House, 1992), 144.

6. Gregory J. Reed, *Economic Empowerment Through the Church* (Grand Rapids: Zondervan, 1994), 11.

Chapter Five: Ministry in African-American Churches

1. Gregory J. Reed, *Economic Empowerment Through the Church* (Grand Rapids: Zondervan), 1994, 145.

2. C. Eric Lincoln and Lawrence H. Mamiya, *The Black Church in the African American Experience* (Durham, N.C.: Duke University Press, 1990), 144.

3. St. Clair Drake and Horace R. Cayton, *Black Metropolis: A Study of Negro Life in a Northern City* (New York: Harcourt Brace, 1945): as quoted in Lincoln and Mamiya, *The Black Church in the African American Experience*, 146.

4. George Barna, *The Power of Vision* (Ventura, Calif.: Regal, 1992), 59.

5. Ibid., 69.

6. Tony Evans, *Let's Get to Know Each Other* (Nashville: Thomas Nelson, 1995), 104.

7. Ibid., 105.

Chapter Six: Contemporary Preaching in African-American Churches

1. In Gayraud S. Wilmore, ed., *African American Religious Studies* (Durham, N.C.: Duke University Press, 1989), 360.

2. Ibid., 156.

3. "Is Min. Farrakhan a Messiah?" *The Final Call* (14 May 1996): 17.

4. Cone, James H., *God of the Oppressed* (New York: Harper & Row, 1975), 226–27.

5. Rosalind Muhammad, "Christian Pastors Defend Min. Farrakhan," *The Final Call* (14 May 1996): 2.

Chapter Seven: Mission Emphases of African-American Churches

1. Gayraud S. Wilmore, *Black America and the Black Radicalism: An Interpretation of the Religious History of Afro-American People* (Maryknoll, N.Y.: Orbis), 108.

2. Richard Gray, "The Black Manifest Destiny Motivation for Mission During the Golden Age of Black Nationalism" (Ph.D. diss., Fuller Institute, 1996), 138–49.

Chapter Eight: Sociological Perspectives of the African-American Church

1. Tariq K. Muhammad, "From Here to Infinity," *Black Enterprise* (June 1996): 141.

2. Quoted in C. Eric Lincoln and Lawrence H. Mamiya, *The Black Church in the African American Experience* (Durham, N.C.: Duke University Press, 1990), 2.

3. Ibid., 319.

4. Quoted in ibid., 8.

5. Quoted in ibid., 16.

Chapter Nine: Economic Factors in African-American Churches

1. Marjorie Whigham-De'sir, "The Real Black Power," *Black Enterprise* (July 1996): 60.

2. Gregory J. Reed, *Economic Empowerment Through the Church* (Grand Rapids: Zondervan, 1994), 145.

3. C. Eric Lincoln and Lawrence H. Mamiya, *The Black Church in the African American Experience* (Durham, N.C.: Duke University Press, 1990), 231, 337.

4. Quoted in George and Yvonne Abatso, *The African American Family* (Chicago: Urban Ministries, 1991), 213–15.

Chapter Ten: The Hostility Factor in the African-American Community

1. Floyd B. Barbour, ed., *The Black Seventies* (Boston: Porter Sargent, 1970), 69.

2. Ibid., 69–70.

3. Walter A. McCray, *Black Young Adults* (Chicago: Black Light Fellowship, 1992), 72.

4. Cornel West, *Keeping the Faith* (New York: Routledge, 1993), 255.

5. Cornel West, *Race Matters* (New York: Vintage Books, 1993), 146–47.

Chapter Eleven: The Homogeneous Principle in African-American Churches

1. For further discussion of E–0 to E–3 evangelism, see Robert E. Logan, *Beyond Church Growth* (Tarrytown, N.Y.: Revell, 1989).

2. C. Peter Wagner, *Church Growth State of the Art* (Wheaton: Tyndale House, 1986), 291.

3. C. Eric Lincoln and Lawrence H. Mamiya, *The Black Church in the African American Experience* (Durham, N.C.: Duke University Press, 1990), 24.

4. Ibid., 50.

5. Montgomery W. Smith, "Homogeneity and American Church Growth" (Ph.D. diss., Fuller Institute, 1976), 49.

6. C. Peter Wagner, *Leading Your Church to Growth* (Ventura, Calif.: Regal, 1984), 34.

7. John T. Sisemore, *Church Growth Through the Sunday School* (Nashville: Broadman, 1983), 31.

Chapter Twelve: The Future of Church Planting in African-American Churches

1. Leith Anderson, *A Church for the 21st Century* (Minneapolis: Bethany House, 1992), 234.

2. Joe S. Ratliff and Michael J. Cox, *Church Planting in the African-American Community* (Nashville: Broadman Press, 1993), 75.

3. Charles W. Walz, "Church Planting and the Mission of the Church" (Ph.D. diss., Fuller Institute, 1984), 76–86.

4. George and Yvonne Abatso, *The African American Family* (Chicago: Urban Ministries, 1991), 29.